Jesus and Philosophy

Jesus and Philosophy

Don Cupitt

scm press

Published in 2009 by SCM Press
Editorial office
13–17 Long Lane,
London, EC1A 9PN, UK

SCM Press is an imprint of Hymns Ancient and Modern Ltd (a reg-
istered charity)
St Mary's Works, St Mary's Plain,
Norwich, NR3 3BH, UK
www.scm-canterburypress.co.uk

British Library Cataloguing in Publication data

A catalogue record for this book is available
from the British Library

978 0 334 04338 6

Typeset by Regent Typesetting, London
Printed in the UK by
CPI Antony Rowe, Chippenham SN14 6LH

Contents

In memory of
Bob Funk

The Divine Image

To Mercy, Pity, Peace, and Love
All pray in their distress;
And to these virtues of delight
Return their thankfulness.

For Mercy, Pity, Peace, and Love
Is God, our father dear,
And Mercy, Pity, Peace, and Love
Is Man, his child and care.

For Mercy has a human heart,
Pity a human face,
And Love, the human form divine,
And Peace, the human dress.

Then every man, of every clime,
That prays in his distress,
Prays to the human form divine,
Love, Mercy, Pity, Peace.

And all must love the human form,
In heathen, turk, or jew;
Where Mercy, Love, & Pity dwell
There God is dwelling **too.**

William Blake

Preface

This book is an attempt to right an historic wrong – or at least, to fill a rather surprising gap. Around 20 years or so after his death, the fiery and very interesting Jewish teacher Jesus of Nazareth began to be idolized by his own followers. Like the Buddha, he was made into the personification of his own teaching, and given an exalted cosmic status. Within a few decades he had been so completely buried by supernatural beliefs about himself that in all the years since, it has been very difficult to make out his own voice, and quite impossible to take him seriously as a thinker. Like royalty, gods are not to be taken seriously: they are to be praised just for being there.

Matters were made even worse when the few surviving good traditions of Jesus' teaching were supplemented by quantities of newly invented and highly tendentious material, and the whole embedded in almost entirely fictional biographies.

Nietzsche greatly feared this worst of all fates, but largely escaped it himself. Karl Marx suffered it, but today with the decay of communism there is a chance that he may be rehabilitated. In Germany, there are already signs of a renewed interest in him.

In the case of Jesus, the critical kind of thinking that is the West's greatest asset has by now broken down the vast dogmatic superstructure built over him, and has gradually refined our successive attempts to recover his original message. Furthermore, it has also changed our moral philosophy and created a new climate in which it has become easier to hear him. We can now at last ask ourselves: Can the original

Jesus, after Christianity, stand on his own feet as a major figure in the history of ethics? Is the long-dead historical Jesus
now of more interest to us than the risen divine Christ that
he was made into?

For the chapters in this book I have made use of the work
of such leading contemporary scholars as Geza Vermes,[1] E. P.
Sanders[2] and John Dominic Crossan.[3] Particularly useful has
been the work of the late R. W. Funk and the Jesus Seminar.[4]
It was done very thoroughly, with the materials, the method,
and the criteria of judgement all quite transparent. Despite
the (perhaps envious) criticism of some haughty Europeans,
I have consulted them constantly, and have disagreed with
them only occasionally. I quote nothing as from Jesus except
material to which they gave a *red* or *pink* coding, the idea
being that this policy brings us at least a generation closer
to the original Jesus than our canonical Gospels, which are
(frankly) a bit of a muddle. An alternative and perhaps equally good policy would have been simply to stick to Q; but unfortunately we do not have a sufficiently coherent and agreed
reconstruction of Q that I can quote.

Q, it should be said in parenthesis here, is the term used
by Gospel critics to describe a hypothetical sayings-Gospel,
written somewhere between the years 50 and 70 CE, and
drawn upon extensively by both Matthew and Luke.[5] When
in the late 1950s the Coptic version of the *Gospel of Thomas*
became available, it too turned out to be a sayings-Gospel.
Together with a few other scraps of evidence, Q and *Thomas*
suggest that the earliest Gospels were sayings-collections,
with very little narrative or biographical material.

Jesus, then, was originally not the Saviour, nor the Messiah,
but simply a moral teacher. Sometimes his sayings were
accompanied by symbolic actions, such as touching the sick
or holding open meals, which were like enactments of his message. He believed there could be, there must be – and perhaps
that there soon *would* be – a world in which human beings
simply accepted each other, without the wariness, the rivalry,
the disdain, the enmity, the suspicion, the envy, the lust, and

the repugnance that are everywhere typical first responses to another person. For his earliest followers, something of Jesus' own charisma still attached to his words, and from the 50s there began the elaborate process of supernaturalizing Jesus' person, his life and his religious status. The sayings-Gospels were developed into narrative Gospels, Jesus' healing touch became the performance of healing-*miracles*, his open meals foreshadowed the Church's Eucharist, and so on. Jesus became, first the Messiah, and then a risen, exalted, heavenly, and eventually even coequally divine figure, an Incarnate Lord and a cosmic King and Saviour.

These developments were not arbitrary. They amounted to an admission that the full realization of Jesus' ethical vision within history was not at present possible, and had been postponed. Meanwhile, he was waiting offstage in the supernatural world, until the moment when he was scheduled to return to earth to establish his kingdom. But the generations went by, until the Church had been waiting vigilantly for so long that it forgot what it was waiting for, and began to treat itself as 'indefectible' and its dogmas as 'immutable'. This idolatry of itself broke the Church's last remaining link with the historical Jesus, and in the long run is proving fatal to it.

That is all water under the bridge by now. Here we try to understand what the original Jesus was on about, and to assess his place in the history of ethics.

I am not at all a New Testament scholar, and this book is written from the point of view of an ethical theorist, or moral philosopher. I'm asking: Is Jesus a figure of real intellectual interest? He was obviously not himself a philosopher, nor was he what we would call a critical thinker. He was a rather secular moral teacher, an Eastern sage, a teacher of wisdom. But did he contribute something unique about morality to our tradition, something that stays with us, and will stay with us even after Christianity has gone? Yes, I think he did. He was the most important pioneer in antiquity of a kind of radical humanism in ethics that is still up to date and challenging even today.

Many people will say that we do not know enough, with enough certainty, about the teaching of Jesus to justify this book's method and conclusions, and it is indeed true that traditional Plato-to-Kant Western philosophy always supposed itself to be dealing with a world of *a priori* truths of reason, and would have been very unhappy about basing a philosophical argument upon merely historical – and therefore merely probable – premises.

In reply, I say that the whole of our knowledge of the human world prior to the invention of printing rests upon physical evidence that will always be open to various interpretations, and manuscript evidence that is always some steps away from the original holograph. All our historical knowledge is fallible, but since the human life-world – a fluid, everchanging and multiperspectival world – is now all we have and all we'll ever have, human philosophy simply ought not to be too puritanical. Compare the evidence for Jesus and his message with the available evidence for Muhammad and for the Buddha. Few people doubt that we have a reasonably clear view of what the latter two great figures were all about. In the case of Jesus, it is true, there is the extra difficulty that layer upon layer of theological interpretation of him was superimposed relatively early on. But when all that is stripped away, Jesus' core message turns out to be not so very different from what many ordinary people have long supposed it to have been.

So I believe we have enough to go on: enough to support my main contention, that at the beginning of Christian tradition there was an extraordinary innovation in ethics. It involved a shift from realism to emotivism, as the moral standard itself was brought down from heaven and relocated in the world of human feelings and relationships, the world of 'the heart'.

Some early readers of this book have wondered why I never mention two of the most popular summaries of Jesus' teaching, namely 'The Lord's Summary of the Law' in two great commandments (Mark 12.29–31 and parallels), and the closely related 'Golden Rule' (Q/Luke 6.31 = Q/Matthew 7.12; cf. *Gospel of Thomas* 6.3). In these sayings, the early

Church pictures Jesus as quoting Scripture, his own contemporary Hillel, and popular wisdom. But the sayings do not express Jesus' own teaching, because they confirm rational self-love, and they tend to assimilate love to justice. Accordingly they were graded only grey (the third grade) by the Jesus Seminar, do not get into *The Gospel of Jesus*, and are not further discussed here. As Jesus reportedly puts it: 'If you do good to those who do good to you, what merit is there in that?' (*Gospel of Jesus* 7.4; Q/Luke 7.33). In his view, it is essential that we should think and love beyond mere reciprocity – as I'll be saying at some length.

D.C.
Cambridge, 2009

The Priority of Ethics

'Life's a wretched business,' said Schopenhauer, making up his mind, 'I have decided to spend mine trying to understand it.'

I like that, but I have never fully shared Schopenhauer's pessimism. Along with his successors Thomas Hardy and Sigmund Freud, he believed that 'dark, unloving forces govern human destiny'. They have us trapped, so that 'man is a squirrel in a cage'. But that was never my own opinion. Even in early adolescence I think I already inclined to the view that is embedded in ordinary language, namely that 'life's what you make it'. Both optimism and pessimism tend strongly to be self-fulfilling, which makes ordinary people wisely prefer to 'look on the bright side' and 'make the best of it'. For us, our current world-picture is in effect the only world there is, and the perceived basic facts of life are the same for everyone, so that if we have a free choice in the matter, then it is altogether more sensible to get yourself into the habit of regarding the glass as being half-full, rather than complaining that it looks half-empty. No *facts* are at issue: we can build the kind of life for ourselves that we want by the attitude we take up.

Do you see why at the age of 14 or so I took this notably idealist view? It is because at that age the adolescent's newly awakened and very intense self-consciousness not only gets one interested in philosophy (what am I? we ask) but also is so strong that consciousness seems to overflow, to spread over the whole world and almost *engulf* it. One is inclined (perhaps like Hamlet?) to *equate* one's own *being* with one's own subjective *consciousness*, and even to equate being with consciousness generally.

Maybe; but if you are one of the many people who speculated in this vein when you were young, and wondered what we are, what life is, how we should live it, and what we should aim for, you will probably accept the idea that ethical and religious questions have a certain priority for us all. You may very well, like my own younger self, tend to give your pursuit of these questions something like a *narrative* shape: our life is (or should be made into) a journey through life towards the goal of life. The ancients commonly saw the philosopher as a traveller, a wandering teacher, and his teaching as guidance for life.

So it was with me. At the age of 15 I found life a puzzle. I wanted to understand it, so that I could find my own place in it, and feel at ease with it. Such questioning led me first to the study of biology, very much as today it leads many other young people to the study of psychology. Then I moved on to theology, and to the philosophy of religion. As the decades have gone by my insistent doubts have gradually made me more sceptical, until I began to reformulate my project. I now wanted to write a fully truthful book about religion, the first ever. I wanted to shed all illusions and self-deception. Before I die, I wanted to look the truth about the human condition full in the face, coolly and without being terrified by it, and having done that I wanted to be able to say Yes to life, living it to the full and making the best of what remains of it for as long as I have it. If I can do this, I will have come to terms with transience. I will have become more than just a passive victim of our common fate, which means that as over the years I have come somewhat closer to Schopenhauer's view of the human condition, I have come to see my task as one, not of sharing, but of overcoming his pessimism. I don't see our life as governed by 'dark unloving forces', in Freud's phrase, but I do see it as 'baseless, brief, pointless and utterly contingent, and yet in its very nihility beautiful, ethically-demanding, solemn and final'. That was written in 1989; more recently I have coined the word 'bitterbittersweet'.

Plato long ago divided philosophy into three great domains, Logic, Physics and Ethics, dealing respectively with the worlds of reason, of fact, and of morality. In a broad sense Ethics includes the whole of *human* philosophy, that is, the philosophies of life, art, religion, politics and morality – which is everything that Bertrand Russell called 'edifying philosophy' and sharply repudiated. Russell in about 1900 committed British analytical philosophy for the next century to Plato's Logic and Physics – that is, to philosophical logic and to the analysis of our empirical knowledge. But I have obstinately gone the other way. *Human* philosophy: that's what nearly all of us started from, and it is what remains most important to us. On the European mainland people who think as I do are sometimes called 'religious existentialists'. Logicians may think and write philosophical logic as if they were pure rational intelligences, and natural philosophers (or scientists as we now call them) may pretend to be disengaged observers who peer into the world from a point outside it; but we devotees of 'human philosophy' are mere talking animals, human beings with an *interest* in life. We need to form a view of what we are, of how we are set or situated in our world as agents, and of how we should live and to what end. As the jargon nowadays has it, we need a 'narrative', a story to live by and to live *out*.

So I like ethics. It was the topic of some of the earliest of all my publications, two essays written in 1961 at a time when I was still fairly young (though not published until 1975), and when in 1962 I returned to Cambridge as a teacher I immediately found myself having to prepare lectures on Christian Ethics. Over the years since, I have not ceased to think that ethics is central to philosophy, but I have also learnt that ethics is only too often a dull and infuriating subject, and disappointing to students, because it is clogged up with obsolete vocabulary and arguments that no longer mean anything to us. Why is ethics in such an unsatisfactory state?

2

What is Wrong with Ethics?

Why then is ethics dull, and why is it such hard work dragging students through the standard series of texts, and the standard arguments for the various ethical theories?

Part of the answer is simply that for all sorts of historical reasons we find ethics difficult to think about clearly. In science we learn about substances and species, their anatomies, their properties, their relationships, their behaviour, all in a neatly classified and tabulated way. That's easy. But in ethics, as in drama, we are trying to follow and understand the complex shifting texture of human relationships. How do words change things? What *is* the 'action' of a drama? What is the relation between selfhood and time? I know I could never write even a half-decent play. A bird book is easy, with its relatively fixed natures and its neatly tabulated layout, whereas the way things change as a small group of people talk together is very difficult indeed to follow. And, to apply all this to ethics, whereas in the past it was considered possible to present an ethical system as a neatly tabulated and codified system of fixed laws, a 'moral theology' perhaps, with notes about casuistry, penalties, and the like, today in everyone's experience moral questions are always deeply *embedded* in the flux of contemporary manners, fashions, culture and personal relationships. Legal thinking, applying a fixed legal code to human lives, may be relatively easy; but human selfhood, expression, action and interaction *in time*, and which in addition are also culturally *embedded*, are hard.

The point needs to be developed further. In the past moral principles were commonly seen as laws. An earthly absolute monarch might promulgate a body of laws, and his officers would enforce them. To this day an offence is a crime against, not the victim, but the *sovereign*, the Crown, in whose name the charge is brought and tried and punished. Similarly, in the Jewish, Christian, and Islamic traditions God is seen as absolute Monarch at the cosmic level. His will for his creation is expressed in natural law, in the natural moral law, and in a body of revealed divine moral commandments. Against such a background all major moral wrongdoing was regarded as sin against *God*, rather than as an offence against a wronged *fellow human*. It was not the *neighbour* whom you had to worry about. He, or she, might not be in any position to do much about your sin, whereas *God* was certainly the one chiefly offended and the one with all the power to detect and punish your sin. It was therefore above all necessary to confess all your sins very frequently to God, and not to your neighbour, and to obtain absolution from God, and not from your neighbour; and that is exactly what believers did. In my own Church general confessions of sin to God were provided at all the principal services in the daily round of worship, but few people even thought of seeking forgiveness from their wronged neighbours. Only in the second half of the twentieth century were most Roman Catholic and other Western service books revised to incorporate the modern sense that many of our sins are sins against our neighbours and perhaps against society generally, as well as against God.

A consequence of all this is that most writing about ethics – at least in the Christian and Muslim worlds, and perhaps in most other places, too – has in the past always been dominated by the models of cosmic law, revealed divine commandments, and religious law generally. The whole moral realm belonged to God, or at any rate to religion, and it was described in legal terms. All the principles of morality added up to a single systematic code in which God had published his unchanging will for us. The moral as such was One, *sui generis* (in a class of its own), immutable and *commanding*. Human beings had been made capable of recognizing it, and of living good and law-abiding lives. Rooted in the eternal world, the principles of morality had to be recognized and applied to the small details of one's own daily life. This was the work of *conscience*.

All these ideas are still very much alive in our own time, when the world is full of people – especially males – who observe their local version of religious law in full and therefore consider themselves to be, morally, very superior persons indeed, while yet being quite unaware of what their daily treatment of many of their fellow humans looks like to others.

In western Europe a long process of secularization began during the later Middle Ages. Secular kingship and court life in Italy, and secular family and business life among the merchant class in northern Europe, as they developed, began to move away from the old church morality and to fill the gap by looking to classical writers for an account of how secular life – in marriage, or at court – should be lived. People learned from Aristotle, the Stoics, and 'humanism'. Modern philosophy then began to develop new moral theories independent of religion. Inevitably they were strongly influenced by the classics, but they also felt that in order to retain credibility they must stick to the pattern of the old religious models – to such an extent that to this day much or most purportedly secular moral thinking in the West remains residually theological. Especially in the rationalist tradition the philosopher had to find and demonstrate a supreme principle of morality, One, *sui generis*, set over us and binding or obliging us all. Moral laws were unchanging and unconditionally obliging, and one spoke of morality in a quasi-religious vocabulary – *duty, obligation, right, conscience, the moral law* – which continued in use up to Sir David Ross in the early twentieth century, and even beyond.

Rationalist moral philosophy, especially of the kind that culminated in Kant, is obviously the ghost of Protestant theology, but other influential modern theories – Aristotelian, utilitarian, and others – have also been heavily influenced by ancient prescientific and religious ways of thinking. They take us back into a world of fixed natures, in which each thing naturally gravitates towards its own appointed 'good'. A moral order was (sort of) built into the world. Moral properties were objective, but being 'non-natural' they were intuited, rather than directly perceived by the senses. And so on: even in these more secularized theories there still remains a strongly felt attachment to moral *realism*, and a mortal terror of the pantomime villain 'relativism'. The basic principles of morality had to remain objective and supra-historical. Like treasure in heaven, they resist the moth and rust of historical change.

Curious: once again we see what a long way Western thought has travelled since the fourteenth century, and at the same time how very slowly and reluctantly it has gradu-ally given up the Graeco-Jewish theological ways of thinking from which it began. Even Derrida still clung on to an 'unde-constructible' idea of justice, I guess because he was reluctant himself to go through moral nihilism. But one consequence of the long domination of moral theory by theology is that it has produced too many tiresomely self-righteous people who neglect their neighbours. One can only too easily keep all the rules, and yet be a rather cold fish.

3

The Hinge of Ethics

In the Western tradition we have in the past been very strongly committed to moral realism. It's very important that one should be *serious* about morality, and to be serious about morality you must, it is said, be an objectivist about moral truth and the moral order. The Latin *mos, mores,* and its equivalent in Greek, *ethos, ethica* did at first mean just customs, 'the done thing' in a particular society. But in our understanding of the term, morality has become much more than that – so much more that nowadays there are still many people who would not dare to think of themselves as being *entitled* to change morality. On the contrary, the moral order is just *there*, One, unchanging, exalted above us, prior to us, *sui generis*, and sacrosanct. Duty is 'the stern daughter of the voice of God', and that's that.

We are all of us, surely, in a general way well aware that behind this sacredness and untouchability of the specifically moral there must lie a long history. Morality – or at least, people's understanding of it – surely has developed, and we can guess roughly how: among us humans some patterns of behaviour have been found convenient, timesaving, and generally peaceable. Such behaviours become habits, individual habits when copied become social customs, customs become traditions, and the whole body of our traditions eventually becomes Holy Tradition, revealed Divine Law, not one bit of which can be altered in any way. This divine law has been codified, interpreted, and applied to life by a zealous army of learned religious professionals. Since nobody can deny that all traditions must have had an historical origin, they must surely have developed in some such way as this; but the suspicion that morality, like religion, has evolved historically does not seem to diminish either its authority or the reverence that we feel for it. On the contrary, it is still as much a duty as ever to 'stand fast in the old ways' and go on venerating and doing what we have (sort-of) 'always' venerated and done. And perhaps it is through this history that God has progressively revealed the moral order to us, just as in the history of religion he is held to have progressively revealed himself more and more fully.

Morality thus understood is clearly the ghost of religion, and 'moral experience' is constructed as the ghost of 'religious experience'.[6] The Voice of conscience is the Early Iron Age 'voice of God', rationalized and universalized now, but still keeping much of its old numinous authority. It is peremptory, commanding, imperative. Very few of our European thinkers gave up any of their religion lightly, and this residually theological way of thinking and feeling about morality has been clung to tenaciously – especially by many people in the older generation – right up to the present day. I guess it now means little to the young, but it is not quite dead yet.

What after all is the alternative to it? In the British tradition it was the seemingly sceptical views of Hobbes and Mandeville that prompted a great flood of writing about moral philosophy during the whole of the eighteenth century.[7] They were felt to be moral cynics, for whom morality is in the end only human, reflecting human feeling-responses and often much less unselfish than it pretends to be. As a child I was taught the businessman's career strategy: 'Get on, get onner, get honest.' First he makes a pile of money, and then he becomes a philanthropist and gets his knighthood. There is a good deal in Bernard Shaw that reflects this view of morality as a figleaf applied by the very successful to dignify themselves and hide the unedifying story of their own climb to wealth and public esteem.

When the eighteenth-century moral philosophers composed their replies to Hobbes and Mandeville they were trying to justify 'the morality of morality', as Nietzsche calls it. They were soon seen to fall into two schools. The *rationalists* stuck to the residually theological view of morality that we have been discussing. The other party defended morality by appealing to our human 'social affections', feelings of the heart, sympathy, benevolence, and so forth – and for their pains they were often derided as *sentimentalists*. Today, they would be called 'emotivists', because even today the suspicion remains that if you don't see morality as being objective, unchanging, and exalted above us – in a word, if you don't hold a (sort-of) theological view of morality – then you are some kind of social subversive, a weak subjectivist, a corrupter of youth, and perhaps (worst of all) a 'relativist'.

Now we see why modern moral philosophy is boring. For two or three centuries we've been stuck in an old controversy that refuses to die down or go away, between a residually theological and disciplinarian view of the moral order, which is distinctly cold-hearted and untrue to our own experience of life but which still somehow manages to cling to the high ground, and a more sociable ethic of the heart and human fellow-feeling, which continues to be derided as weak, soppy and – worst of all – *liberal*. We are stuck with this controversy. To find the hinge of ethics, the crux that makes the subject really interesting, we must not evade this perennial dispute. We must sharpen it up. I suggest that the most interesting and important moment in moral thinking is the moment when a courageous individual suddenly rebels against the long overshadowing and indeed the domination of the moral life and of ethical theory by religious authority. This brave individual paradoxically attempts a moral critique of what in his society currently passes for morality – and then, realizing the paradox of what he or she is doing, goes further and attempts outright to expropriate God and seize morality for us humans. Morality is ours. We made it, and we can change it. It is for us, and not we for it.

This thrilling and terrifying moment of life-or-death violent struggle between humankind and God for the ownership of the moral realm and the right to revise it *in the human interest* is so prominent in the Hebrew Bible that it is remembered as the very meaning of the name Isra-el, 'the One who strives with God'. Stories about the *chutzpah*, the shameless audacity, that challenges God ethically are told in connection with Jacob, Abraham, Job, Jeremiah and many others. In the New Testament period and later, the decision *not* to impose observance of the Jewish Law upon gentile converts could be read, and by many was read, as asserting that the new Christian ethic of mutual *human* love and forbearance had in a radical way fulfilled, displaced, and made quite redundant the old ethics of revealed divine Law. At least some Christians of unimpeachable orthodoxy, such as Augustine of Hippo, said as much in so many words: *Dilige et quod vis fac* (Love, and do what you will). Indeed, in the whole story of the emergence of Christianity from Judaism there is, from the ancients to Freud, an undercurrent that recognizes the new faith as having arisen from a humanistic revolt against God. Remember that Lucifer is a title *both* of Christ *and* of Satan, two characters who in iconography look startlingly alike. Jesus was a rebel who bore God's punishment for our sakes. So he redeemed us from God. That is the subtext that must be kept in the dark. Forget what I just said.

The battle between so-called 'deontological' ethical theories – by which is meant residually theological ethical theories built around ideas of law and conscience, duty and obligation: theories, in short, that model the relationship to morality upon the relation to God – and humanistic ethical theories, built around ideas of human love, benevolence, happiness, sympathy, the social affections and so on, has repeatedly cropped up in modern times. Indeed it is perhaps the only area of philosophy to which the dim English have made a major contribution. Here I briefly mention, first, the transition from liberal Puritanism to early humanitarianism in John Locke and his pupil the third Earl of Shaftesbury, around the year 1700; second, the best and most dazzling

lines of William Blake, together with some of the young
Wordsworth, around the year 1800; and third, the first
generation of post-Darwinian (and even post-*Nietzschean*)
writers, figures such as George Bernard Shaw, D. H. Lawrence
and Oscar Wilde, around 1900.

Evidently we have to do here with a perennial controversy,
revived in new forms generation after generation. On one side
we have the claim that wild, rebellious human nature needs to
be constrained by an objective and authoritative code of Law.
Religious and moral conservatives are Hobbesians, believers
in the necessity of strong government. Here all the interest is
in the *vertical* relation, through conscience, of the individual
to the moral standard; the individual's iron self-control and
driving will. On the other side, there is the claim that 'love
is the fulfilling of the law'. The horizontal relation to the
neighbour is sufficient. Human beings are social, and find
their chief happiness through their 'social affections' – sympathy, benevolence, kindness or fellow-feeling, and love. Did
not our religious tradition promise all along that the hoped-
for Better World would come when the divine Law and the
divine Spirit have been fully internalized within the human
heart? We will have finally become human beings when we
have entirely given up objective, heteronomous ethics and
have learnt instead simply to live by the heart.

To this, those who continue to uphold ethical theories of the
old deontological and residually theological type have always
the same reply. They are on the political and disciplinarian
Right. They are moral objectivists or realists. They believe in
the Law of the Father, and they expect to see it stringently
enforced. They are utterly convinced that they alone occupy,
always have occupied, and always will occupy the moral high
ground, and they always have derogatory terms for the view
opposed to theirs. As we have seen, in the eighteenth century
they described the ethics of human sympathy as 'sentimental-
ism', and in the twentieth century used the word 'emotivism'.
A whole group of words such as 'philanthropic', 'humane',
and 'humanitarian' were for a very long time used chiefly in

a derogatory sense by people on the hardnosed Right, wor-
shippers of a cruelly authoritarian God. Then, about twenty
years ago, the word 'humanitarian' suddenly overcame its
own long history – more than a century – of being used as
equivalent to 'bleeding-heart liberal' or 'do-gooder'. When
thinking about the claims of moral realism and its lofty pre-
tensions to objectivity and rationality, we need also to bear
in mind its ruthlessly dirty tricks with language, and its sheer
ugliness. When you hear people prating about morality and
'the difference between right and wrong', start counting your
spoons. They are all potential crooks.

I am suggesting, then, that to make ethics interesting again
we need to sharpen up and to make central the controversy
that I believe is still the hinge of ethics today. The 'right wing'
view emphasizes our 'vertical' relationship to the Moral
Standard, seen as being real, unchanging, and authoritative.
It is the Law, known by conscience. It calls for conscientious
and dutiful discharge of our obligations, for an iron will and
for strict self-control. On this view the relation to one's fellow
human being is secondary. The neighbour is merely the one
to whom or for whom we do our duty, and that is all. He or
she exists chiefly to increase my own conviction of my own
righteousness.

So much for the residually theological ethics of people who
are usually found on the political Right, or alternatively are
themselves observant followers of a religion that sees the
moral life in terms of obedience to a revealed code of religious Law. The alternative view puts all the emphasis upon
the 'horizontal' relationship to the fellow human. Its organ of
moral knowledge is not the conscience, but rather the heart.
It sums up the two chief commandments of the Law, love God
and love your neighbour, in the *second*, because this moral
outlook is non-metaphysical. Everything has come down
into the 'horizontal' temporally flowing world of human life,
which is now seen as the field of morality and of human feeling. Self-transcendence is now not a matter of conscientiously
living under a Law that is imposed upon one from Above,

but rather of a heightened self-awareness that enables us to recognize and to shake off all those things in ourselves that make it difficult for us to love and be loved freely.

4

The Rebel

I have drawn a sharp distinction between a type of ethical theory that defines the moral life in terms of one's relation to an objective and lawlike moral standard of overriding authority, variously described as God, as divine law, as the moral law, as practical reason, as a categorical imperative, or even as some kind of natural objective 'fittingness'; and another type of ethical theory that has arisen in protest against it, and which is deliberately non-objective, being based on nothing more substantial than ordinary human fellow-feeling. The first sort of ethic values obedience, the will and strict *control*; the second sort of ethic is thoroughly anthropocentric and emotivist. It defines the moral life in terms of the way you relate to your fellow human being. It simply does without any external authority, and declares that all you need is love, or that 'the milk of human kindness' is a sufficient basis for ethics.

The two ethical theories are in more or less perennial contention. Consider a topic such as the raising of children: the first type of ethic says that children are born wild, and need to be socialized by discipline, training and the setting of firm boundaries, whereas the second type of ethic says that all you need to do with children is to give them some space, stop pushing them too hard and instead be consistently loving to them, and they will be fine. John Locke's celebrated essay on education took – or at least approached – this latter view, opening the way to the 'child-centred' approach to education that remains standard liberal policy (and enrages conservatives) to this day.

But when, we may wonder, did the 'subjective' or humanistic approach to morality begin? In a notable recent book, the distinguished American historian of ideas Gertrude Himmelfarb[8] has, I think correctly, argued that the distinctive and most important contribution of the British Enlightenment, publishing in London and Edinburgh, lay in the field of ethics, together with 'political economy' and the beginnings of modern social thought generally. Nor was the achievement of the period limited to the publishing of books, for it also saw the pioneering of a very wide range of new social initiatives, reforming, philanthropic, and libertarian. Many of the new social initiatives were indeed of the traditional 'top-down' kind, which involved very rich people subscribing to establish an institution that would care for some group of poor and needy folk, but there were also other and newer kinds of initiative. Some campaigns sought and obtained *changes in the law* and so aided the development of the modern ethically active state. Other movements such as Methodism had in them a large and important element of *self-help*, as ordinary folk learnt how to organize themselves, 'improve' themselves, and make themselves respectable. This prepared the way for labour unions and a large-scale working-class movement in later times.

Very well: but what made possible the emergence of this new and strongly humanistic ethic of philanthropic feeling, social reform and self-improvement? The familiar answer is surely the correct one: the triumph of the new mechanistic world-picture in the work of Newton suddenly made the universe seem very chilly and non-human. There is no purposiveness out there, and no readymade moral order built into the way the world goes. All the old 'realist' or objectivist moral theories had suddenly been shown to be just untrue. There is no readymade moral framework, laid on for us at cosmic level, which asks of us only obedient conformity. On the contrary, the universe is cold and non-moral; so cold that we humans find thrust upon us the sole responsibility for building the moral order that we are to live by. Frankly, we've little choice but to 'love one another or die', or, rather more severely: 'we must love one another *and* die'.

That's the truth; but of course nobody could have put it as starkly as that in 1700. On the contrary, writers like Alexander Pope managed to combine enthusiasm for Newton's achievement with untroubled Cosmic Toryism: the whole system of things within which we live remains in his view wisely planned and benevolent, and 'whatever is, is right'. What happened, in moral philosophy as in other and related areas, was that Western thought fought a prolonged rearguard action, clinging to a residually theological moral realism that was getting thinner and thinner. A few leading spirits protested, declaring for atheism and moral nihilism, or (more recently) for straightforward emotivism; but they are offset by an equal or greater number of writers reacting in a neo-conservative direction and battling to reinstate a thoroughgoing ethics of obedience to the revealed Will of God. So the controversy continues, and perhaps most conspicuously in the USA, where it is the single most important faultline that divides civil society and distinguishes the two principal political parties.

Today no doubt most younger people (at least, in Europe) are of the revolutionary-humanist or emotivist party. God is dead, and everything is permitted – at least in the sense that morality is only human, and is evolving steadily through our human conversation. Each new generation regards as commonplace things that shocked and outraged their parents. Such people are bored by all those classic ethical theories that were and still are attempting to explain and justify a residually theological account of morality. Talk of moral judgements as expressing timeless and objective truths is obviously absurd to people who are now only too well aware of how mobile and how fast-changing are the feelings and valuations annexed to each item in the vocabulary of everyday speech. Morality changes all the time, and we are the ones who are changing it, through the way we push words around in our daily conversation with each other. We have no idea of what the limits of future ethical development may be. But so tenacious is our attachment to the old 'theological' model – moral truths as eternal verities – that even today one still hears a few senior moral philosophers being highly indignant with their young students for being such a crowd of unthinking 'relativists', 'subjectivists' and 'sceptics'.

On the view I have been suggesting, it seems that so far as the modern West is concerned the great divide in ethics opened up between about 1690 and 1730. In philosophy, the new human-centred ethic of benevolence or sympathy starts in the relationship of Locke with his pupil Shaftesbury. In society generally, it starts with groups of people like those whom Thomas Coram succeeded in attracting to his project of establishing the first Foundling Hospital (1739) for abandoned babies. A little earlier, Coram had been a trustee of Georgia, which reminds one that a number of the American colonies were actually planned as 'ethical states', several generations *before* humanitarian reforms in West European countries encouraged Kant and Hegel to introduce the idea of the ethical state into European philosophy. In Georgia, as originally planned, there was to be no slavery. At least some of those who organized the first American colonies were going straight from classical Protestantism to an attempt to build a religious-humanist society, the Kingdom of God on earth.

So much for the modern history of the two chief types of ethical theory. One theory sees the moral life in terms of each individual's relation to a transcendent, objective moral standard, and the other type of theory sees the moral life entirely in terms of the 'horizontal' relationship between one human being and the next. One party believes in the government of life by Divine Law, or something like it, and the other party is antinomian. It aims to live by love alone: it yearns for absolute freedom.

But when did this *second* type of ethic first begin? I have been hinting that it derives from the old biblical dream of the future establishment of a fully free and good society on earth at the end of time. In *The Meaning of the West* (2008) I copied out the dozen or so chief passages about this topic that are to be found in the Hebrew Bible. They all describe a world in which the common people enjoy a full span of life, in peace, justice and prosperity. They often see this ethically ideal world as 'Jerusalem', and it does not matter at all whether the new Jerusalem comes into being as a result of long-sustained human strivings, or as the result of a special supernatural intervention from Heaven. What matters is the dream, the dream of a fully liberated human society. In such a society there will be no need of any external religious discipline, nor of any religious mediation. People will then have 'hearts of flesh', *soft* hearts; they will have the divine Spirit within them, or they will have 'the law written on their hearts'; and once again, which of these things you say doesn't matter. All that matters is the indelible ethical dream that one day is going to come true, or rather, make itself come true. And the dream is 'Jerusalem', or in New Testament terms, 'the Kingdom of God'. And, once again, even *God* no longer matters, for in the new Jerusalem God is internalized, and is no longer an objective Sovereign out there. God is so fully internalized that he dies into the individual heart, and is just the 'brightness' and the love between persons that the dream promises.[9]

You see what I'm driving at? The great prophet in antiquity of our modern radical humanist ethic, of our 'subjectivism', our emotivism, our desire to see human beings fully 'free at last' was a neglected Jewish teacher, Jesus of Nazareth. He fell into severe neglect very early, because barely twenty years after his death a great religion began to grow up around his name. From the first, it began to falsify his message: it exalted him to the heavenly world, it made him into the personification of his own teaching, it made of him therefore himself just one more sovereign lawgiver, and around him it rebuilt all the ugly old apparatus of authoritarian, mediated religion – and so eventually it became a standing denial of his original message. But mercifully, a few of his own sayings and ideas survived, including his own *ethical* version of critical thinking; so that the Enlightenment critique of Christianity, as it gradually broke up the gigantic religious ideology built around him, at last began to recover his original message.

At this point we have to consider a large number of obvious objections, for until we have faced them down I have no prospect of carrying you with me any further.

5

Objections Overruled

When, in *Above Us Only Sky*, I set out in brief summary today's version of kingdom-religion, and called it 'The Religion of Ordinary Life', my summary did not include any mention of the name of Jesus of Nazareth. The reason for this is obvious enough: to base one's whole way of life upon historical claims about any person or chain of events in the remote past would be irrational. It would be a kind of religious 'foundationalism' or traditionalism. In the case of Jesus the available evidence from Christian sources canonical and apocryphal, from Jewish sources, and from Greek and Latin classical literature is very diverse and hard to assess. For the foreseeable future it will continue to be possible for critical scholars examining all the material to come up with a wide spectrum of different reconstructions of the historical life and message of Jesus. No one theory of what he was all about can expect to prevail for long – if at all. In the case of *theories in natural science*, experimental work usually ensures that a new theory, if it looks to be of some real interest and sounds plausible, gets checked out and quickly begins either to prevail or to drop into obscurity. Only in a minority of high-level cases that clearly lie beyond any very speedy testing, such as questions concerning the first beginnings of life on Earth, questions in physical cosmology, and similar areas does disagreement persist for several generations. But in *history* there is no experimental falsification – apart, perhaps, from the discovery of really important new arguments or pieces of evidence. Which, unfortunately, is rare. In the case of the quest of the historical Jesus, the twentieth century produced little really important new evidence. The Dead Sea Scrolls, together with the Coptic text of *Thomas* and other texts found at Nag Hammadi in 1945, are about all that we can cite. From them we have learnt only what we have learnt from *Thomas*, namely that there probably were a number of very early sayings-gospels, containing some good traditions of sayings composed by Jesus and by him taught to his followers.

This last point, however, is of real interest. I agree with those who point out that New Testament documents *outside* the canonical Gospels show little knowledge of Jesus' life. This observation consorts well with the suggestion that (as in the case of the Buddha) the earliest 'gospels' were collections of the Teacher's sayings, like the Buddhist *Dhammapada*. Jesus probably taught his followers, and they memorized, a body of short secular-humanist fictional stories (the parables), some hundreds of epigrammatic sayings, and a few brief dialogues with questioners and opponents. The stories and sayings conveyed the special kind of moral insight that concerned him. As for Jesus' *life*, we know next to nothing of it. The gospel as a sort of theologized biography we owe to Mark. He was probably the chief inventor of the genre. His Gospel clearly follows the usual pattern of the life of an ancient oriental holy man, and was constructed in order to show Jesus as fulfilling the scriptures. Mark's narrative seems to reflect the traumatic recent event of the destruction of the Temple in 70 CE, and it seems to include a response to people who were asking why faith in Jesus' messiahship had developed only recently, and was not around in Jesus' lifetime. Jesus, it claims, had wanted his messiahship to be kept secret.

The most we can say about Jesus' life is a string of 'probablys': Jesus lived in the first third of the first century CE. He was born at Nazareth. His parents were probably named Joseph and Mary, and two leaders subsequently prominent in the early Jerusalem Church, namely James and Simon, were probably his brothers. Jesus was a moral teacher, who wandered about Palestine for a few years. His teachings were probably accompanied by some symbolic actions – open common meals, healings, and perhaps also public criticisms of the Jerusalem Temple. The meaning of these symbolic acts was clear to anyone familiar with the similar actions of some of the old Israelite prophets: Jesus was enacting the 'nearness' of the new moral order that he taught. During the early 30s Jesus fell foul of the authorities, and was executed by crucifixion. His person and work were at first not theologized at all by the tiny surviving band of his followers, who preserved only the tradition of his sayings, at first in oral, and then later in written form.

The early sayings-gospels began to be put into written form a generation or so after Jesus' death – no doubt in order to preserve the tradition at a time when Jesus' original disciples were beginning to die off. Thereafter – as *Thomas* seems to show – the written text underwent a good deal of revision and supplementation as it was copied and recopied. But to the modern reader it seems evident that at least one-third of *Thomas* is still early tradition, and of good quality. It is the only apocryphal gospel of which as much can be said.

In summary, we have none of Jesus' very own words (*ipsissima verba*) in his own hand. But we have a great deal of evidence, some of it probably good and early, for his teaching. In that evidence we hear a distinctive individual voice. The most thorough recent review of it all is that carried out by 80 or so Fellows of the 'Jesus Seminar' between 1985 and 1993. David Boulton has a useful summary of their carefully debated criteria and method of assessing and grading the evidence, and then briefly summarizes their conclusions:

> Having examined 1330 reported sayings of Jesus (420 in Matthew, 177 in Mark, 392 in Luke, 140 in John and 210 in Thomas) the Seminar voted 29 red, 184 pink, 381 grey, and 736 black. Of the red [*top grade, DC*] sayings, 11 were found in Q/Matthew, 14 in Q/Luke, 1 in Mark, none in John and 3 in Thomas. Pink [*second grade, DC*] say-

ings broke down as 60 from Q/Matthew or Matthew's M source, 65 from Q/Luke or Luke's L source, 65 from Mark and 40 from Thomas.[10]

All the sayings that picked up the most votes came from Q. They were, says Boulton, Q/Matthew 5.39 ('turn the other cheek'), Q/Matthew 5.40 ('when sued for your coat, give your cloak too'), Q/Luke 6.20 ('blessed are the poor'), Q/Matthew 5.41 ('go the second mile'), and Q/Luke 6.27 ('love your enemies'). This suggests that the ordinary person's hazy impression of Jesus' core message is not far off the mark.

In 1995 Robert W. Funk, the founder of the Jesus Seminar, assembled these results into a very carefully composed *Gospel of Jesus*, which reflects the state of the best available traditions about Jesus as they may have stood in about the year 50 or 60. In this book Jesus' Messiahship does not yet appear, but Funk does include at the end a brief report to the effect that first Mary of Magdala and then Cephas/Peter, and then perhaps some others, with the last of them all being Paul on the Damascus Road, claimed to have had visions of the risen Jesus. (The empty tomb story developed much later.)

Thus *The Gospel of Jesus* represents about the best available attempt to give the reader a vivid impression of the Jesus of the first generation, as he was just before the sudden very large development of Christology in the writing of Paul, Mark and others. Alternatively, a very handy catalogue of Jesus' likeliest sayings is to be found in Funk's *Honest to Jesus*.[11]

He was, of course, a moral teacher: a notably *secular* teacher, who does not appeal to religious law, and in whose core teaching – i.e., the parables – there is remarkably little – indeed almost *no* – supernatural apparatus. I have already suggested that the endlessly debated phrase 'The Kingdom of God' is best understood as having had in late-ancient Jewry very much the same range of associations and uses as 'Jerusalem' in modern rather left-wing English. It is Blake's Jerusalem, the Jerusalem that we are to build in England's green and pleasant land, and it is the Jerusalem of Arnold

Wesker's play *I'm Talking about Jerusalem*, the dream of a good society that inspires old-fashioned leftists. At the same time it is also the New Jerusalem, coming down from heaven as a bride adorned for her husband. It is a secular hope, the age-old dream of a good society here on this earth.

The American version of all this is very similar: 'The Kingdom of God in America' is a dream of all-round freedom and dignity for the ordinary citizen that the Founding Fathers tried to fix for us to inherit; a dream that continues as a guiding ideal in the present and as a future hope.

In *both* cases the much-laboured contrast between a present merely human reality and a great future supernatural hope is unnecessary. The great religious dreams are with us all the time: always present, always coming into being, and always promised.

And that is all there is to say. Those hundreds of learned scholars who have written shelves of books about the meaning for Jesus of the phrase 'the kingdom of God' were largely wasting their time and ours. They were not listening closely enough to the behaviour of religious language in *our own* everyday speech.

Jesus, then, is no sort of religious conservative, and no sort of swivel-eyed apocalyptist. He was a secular moral teacher, battling to raise our moral awareness; battling to get all the negative emotions out of human relationships – and by 'negative emotions' I mean not only 'envy, hatred, malice and all uncharitableness', and not only 'lust, oppression, crime', but much more, for he carries his satirical attack on the ethics of law so far as to ridicule our most basic everyday ideas of justice and desert. Now that really *is* extreme.

6

Against the Law

There is a persistent strain of antinomianism in Christianity: it is already referred to by St Paul, and it has surfaced from time to time ever since. It is very often taken to be the view of those who hold that their experience of divine Grace has been so great that they need not trouble themselves about observing the moral law. They can now 'sin greatly – and yet more greatly believe'. But I don't wish to discuss *that* view here. Rather, I take antinomians to be people who have a very strong sense of the utter moral inadequacy and unsatisfactoriness of the legal model for understanding the moral life. I mean the codification of a system of general moral rules to be observed punctiliously, and the setting up of a finely balanced network of reciprocal duties and their corresponding rights. Human life is to be lived 'by the book', and 'sticking to the rules'. But the antinominian retorts that in practice an ethical code of this kind – variously called 'legalism' and 'the morality system' – is burdensome and oppressive. It does not produce a good and happy society, and never can do so.

It seems that the historical Jesus was strongly antinominian in this latter sense. In the core tradition of his teaching he does not actually *mention* Moses or the Torah at all. Indeed, much of the time he speaks like an Eastern sage, as if he scarcely had any particular and local ethnic or religious affiliation of his own. He refers to the Law only indirectly, by his notably lax attitude to it. He and his disciples nibble corn as they walk through the cornfields on a Sabbath day, and when challenged he produces the famous lines that I here give in Funk's translation:

26

The Sabbath day was created for Adam and Eve,
Not Adam and Eve for the Sabbath day.
So, the son of Adam lords it even over the Sabbath day.[12]

In effect, religious prescriptions are manmade, and we should view them purely instrumentally. Human well-being comes first, as in the healing of a man with a crippled hand in the synagogue, also on the Sabbath. Jesus takes an equally lax view of other laws, too: for example, when he calls his disciples they are required simply to abandon their parents abruptly. Again, his attitude to the regulations for getting into and maintaining a state of ritual purity was notoriously dismissive. And, too, one notes that although menstruation or any kind of haemorrhage in a woman was considered highly polluting, it does not put Jesus off in the least.

Jesus' attitude to the Torah was such that it soon gave rise to the charge that he aimed to destroy the Law altogether. Perhaps he did: but the early Christian communities were very reluctant to go that far. In Matthew 5.17–20 early Jewish Christians ascribe to him the view that the whole Law, every jot and tittle of it, remains binding. There follow a series of 'antitheses' contrasting what was once said (namely, in the Torah), and a rather tightened-up, 'internalized' version attributed to Jesus. Not just killing is prohibited, but anger; not just adultery is prohibited, but lust. Swearing and divorce are bad things – but what Jesus had actually said about divorce was (and still is) a matter of dispute. Laying down general moral rules to serve (presumably) as disciplinary canons for the early Church was in fact completely alien to him. He is no lawgiver, no, not in any way.

But then, suddenly, we are back on firm ground with Jesus' familiar attack on the morality system and its reciprocities:

As you know, we once were told, 'An eye for an eye' and 'A tooth for a tooth'. But I tell you: Don't react violently against the one who is evil: when someone slaps you on the right cheek, turn the other as well. When someone wants to sue you for your shirt, let that person have your coat along with it. Further, when anyone conscripts you for one mile, go an extra mile. Give to the one who begs from you . . .[13]

And so on, with more excellent stuff until the end of the chapter. We are reminded that this ethic of non-violence or non-retaliation (beware of road-rage, and every sort of rage, especially political 'rage'), this ethic of *ahimsa*, proved still to have considerable power in the twentieth century, when it was picked up and used by various major figures such as Tolstoy, Gandhi and Martin Luther King. And its major feature is its refusal to reciprocate *in kind*, to get even. Instead, Jesus asks for acts of ecstatic generosity that disrupt the morality system. He really wants to destroy the ordinary person's ideas about justice as fair shares, and as proportionate retribution.

An anecdote about Kant, the greatest example of a philosopher of the morality system. Kant was of very modest social origins, and had some poor relations. He was a fastidious bachelor, a creature of habit; but he did his duty. He arranged for the payment to his humble relations of a regular allowance. That was his moral duty, and he did it. But otherwise he never saw them: keeping the rules was in his view quite enough.

After 'Christianity' had itself become a religion of law, the moral theologians developed a famous distinction between 'mandates' (Latin, *mandata*, the rules of the pass-standard morality that was binding upon all Christians), and the 'counsels of perfection' (usually calling the believer to vows of total poverty, chastity and obedience), which were for those who wished to aim for a higher standard. The distinction was customarily explained by citing the story of the rich young ruler, who said to Jesus in Matthew 19.16–22 that he had kept all the commandments: what more should he do? Jesus replies: 'If you would be perfect, sell what you possess and give to the poor', and the young man goes away sadly. He is very rich, and this is too much for him. In 1 Corinthians 7 Paul rather similarly writes about virginity as an optional extra for those who want to aim at rather more than the minimum.

So much for the doctrine of supererogation. In Roman Catholic theology the works of supererogation performed by the saints in the past add up to a 'treasury of merit' that can be drawn upon by ordinary folk worried about their sins. By paying an appropriate fee to the authorities at Rome they can draw upon this treasury, and so shorten their time in purgatory.

I will not go any further into the unedifying details of yesterday's theology. For our present purposes, it is enough to ask 'Did the later doctrine of works of supererogation satisfactorily preserve Jesus' insight, that a law-morality that is content to keep all the rules is not enough?'

No, it did not! Jesus' idea was that a morality of law that defines and observes moral rules precisely, that establishes an elaborate network of reciprocal rights and duties, and that says: '*This* is the good life. Keep all these rules punctiliously, even if only for one day, and the Kingdom of God will come' – such a morality is utterly unbearable. We will all be spying on each other, to make sure that nobody is getting away with anything. We'll all be worried that we are insufficiently respected, and like the old hands in the parables we'll find the next person's undeserved good fortune hard to bear. There cannot be a good and humanly fulfilling society unless everyone is willing on occasion to be ecstatically generous, as when someone donates blood, or another organ, to a stranger; or is willing, for example, to go to the aid of a victim of misfortune *anonymously*. A little touch of excess, a little touch of love for the fellow human *just as such*, is essential. Now and again, you must do something for a fellow human whose sex, age, faith, race, nationality and so on you *do not know*. Here we glimpse Jesus' radical humanism, his understanding that morality itself only becomes really moral when human beings have fully appropriated it to themselves. No god can possibly tell me what morality is. Only my own heart can do that. Like 'purity', morality shouldn't be seen as being a matter of what gets put *into* us; it depends upon what comes out of us.

Who came nearest to understanding the point here? William Blake, of course, especially in some of his unpublished lyrics, whereas the Church, by making Jesus into an incarnate god, a cosmocrator and a 'lawgiver', reversed his message and buried him.

7

Contradictions

When, over twenty years ago, the Jesus Seminar embarked upon a fresh appraisal of the evidence for the teaching of Jesus, they defined their criteria of historicity very carefully, and in terms with which I am generally in agreement. But they did miss one trick: what are we to do about the various *conflicts*, or even straight ethical *contradictions*, within the material ascribed to Jesus, especially in cases where the conflict still comes through even in the core-tradition that we have finally arrived at?

The Seminar rightly saw that we should listen out for a forceful, distinctive, early-sounding, pre-Christian, provincial radical (i.e. Galilean) voice. But should we, or should we not, assume that it must have been a *coherent* voice?

Years ago, teaching ethics, I used to ask ethics students to search for obvious contradictions in the teaching ascribed to Jesus in Matthew, Mark and Luke. In the entire history of Christianity hardly anyone has ever had their brain switched on when studying Jesus' teaching. The available literature is poor, so I was attempting to galvanize the unlucky students. To start them off, I pointed out an easy one. In Matthew 6, Jesus exhorts his disciples to practise a piety of what Kierkegaard calls 'hidden inwardness'. You should give alms, pray and fast *secretly*. This is the Platonic piety of those who see the religious life as a hidden 'inner life' of the soul. But in the preceding chapter believers were told to let it all hang out and to make themselves conspicuous. They are like lamps that should be set up on a lampstand so that they can illuminate others: like a hilltop city, they need to be seen. But which was Jesus' view?

With that one example to start with, I sent the students off to find a few more of such contradictions, and then write an essay about them. My own solution to the example just quoted was as follows: the secret, introvertive piety of Matthew 6 could not have originated until the 50s at the very earliest. It presupposes a division of reality into two worlds, an unseen supernatural world above where the risen Jesus sits at the right hand of God, and our everyday, visible world here below in which we continue to live our ordinary bodily lives. But Jesus was a one-world person, a secularizer, a moralist of this life, a composer of fictions and a 'kingdom' man. He could not have commended the later Christian piety of those who think that this life is only half-real and that our 'real' life is a second, secret, inner life of the soul, in which we continually relate ourselves to our real and true home in the eternal world. Jesus was no amphibian (literally, a liver of a double life, between two worlds) and certainly would not have endorsed Kierkegaard's comparison of the believer with a spy, who has a second, hidden, identity. So I presumed that the historical Jesus must have been the expressivist, the postmodern type of person who says that you've got to put on a brave show, because the show is all there is. So, 'Burn, baby, burn!' Let your light shine: be solar. That's Jesus.

Unfortunately, when I came to read *The Gospel of Jesus* closely I found that, contrary to my expectation, it incorporates sayings of both kinds. Another example that surprised me is this: *The Gospel of Jesus* also incorporates conflicting sayings about moneylending. One saying, of the be-ecstatically-generous type, tells us to lend money to, and only to, people whom we know are not going to be able to repay it, just as we should invite to dinner only people who cannot and will not ask us back. But there are other sayings and parables in which Jesus – or at least, the masters in his stories – require us to be prudent investors. More generally we may ask: 'In his ethical teaching at large, is Jesus commending prudence or imprudence?' *Which?* Since prudence is one of the four cardinal virtues in Christian teaching, I have usually assumed that Jesus himself must have been a consistent opponent of it. He would surely have excoriated our 'rational egoism', our 'legitimate concern for our own interest', wouldn't he? In which case, we need to give some account of the sense in which Jesus *does* nevertheless seem to commend worldly prudence.

My present feeling about it all is as follows: Jesus does commend imprudence, because for him we are not ethical beings at all unless we are capable when the occasion calls for it of rising above the law and responding with an immediate, unthinking, 'ecstatic' generosity to a fellow human being in need or distress. Bare co-humanity, the milk of human kindness, is of the essence. It cannot be prescribed for us by any Other: it has to be a spontaneous impulse of the human heart; and in that sense the ethical is purely and only human. But Jesus does not wish to commend irrationality. We should not be 'suckers', easily duped. On the contrary, with his usual ruthless satire, he is quite ready to provoke his own followers by commending those who are smart, fly, streetwise, shrewd, and generally quick on the uptake.

This means that for Jesus ecstatic generosity is not the wet emotionalism of those persons in show business who notoriously are easily moved and not very bright. On the contrary, he stresses, with notable originality, the moral importance of a high level of critical self-consciousness. Get that beam out of *your own* eye, calculate, and *then* be extravagantly generous – because *that* is what breaks the culture of *ressentiment*, melts the heart, and unfreezes human relationships.

On this point, Gandhi understood Jesus correctly, and actually showed the correct and crafty combination of shrewd calculation and moral excess in his own use of non-violence against the powerful. Yes, yes! Gandhi was both dove and serpent, and quite right too. It's a very difficult trick to pull off correctly, but Gandhi knew how to do it.

8

The Blasphemer

The importance of Jesus in the history of ethics, I am suggesting, lies in the fact that he was an early forerunner – and perhaps *the* classical forerunner – of an approach to ethics that we usually regard as being distinctively modern. So modern, in fact, that it remains faintly scandalous in many quarters to this day. Most moral theories are, as they always have been, objectivist. They have always been theological or residually theological in that they have seen morality as being determined by something out-there, which may be called the Will of God, or the natural moral law that is built into the created order, or a code of religious law such as *shariah* or the Torah, or eternal moral verities out-there – or something of the kind; for the list of things out there that may be thought to give to morality its objectivity and its overriding authority over us is very long.

At any rate, to those who hold a view of this type it seems obvious that we humans have no power or authority to question the morality of morality, or to change it in any way. Certainly not: morality is sacrosanct. It is different. It is *sui generis*; it has its own distinctive essence, which moral philosophy investigates. One very popular account of this 'essence' is that it is grammatically imperative.[14] It is commanding. It creates obligation: it *binds* us.

However, at the beginning of the nineteenth century Hegel began to bring the moral order down into history, and to see it as being all tied up in a single package with people's manners, their customs, their *culture*. That is already halfway to thinking of morality as historically evolving and even, dare I say it, as manmade. Ordinary people have today been made familiar with this notion by seeing cinema and television presentations of *costume drama*, in which it becomes obvious that those people's speech, their dress, their moral conventions, their manners, their buildings and so on are all part of a single whole, which has evolved continuously from their day to ours. So it is that our twentieth-century popular mass media have made us all Hegelians by now, even if without the final totalization that Hegel himself looked forward to. Then at the end of the century Nietzsche finally said the obvious by announcing the arrival of moral nihilism – that is, the catastrophic end of all forms, even the most residual, of moral realism. Now we see that it's up to us to create new values, and to rebuild the moral order on a purely human basis, seeing it not as binding the will, but as springing from the heart. In the English-speaking world most people so fear and dislike this new, non-realistic and only-human analysis of morality that they spent the entire twentieth century trying to decry it, label it 'emotivism', and dismiss it as lacking in seriousness.

Nevertheless, the new only-human way of thinking about morality has now prevailed in the common life of people in the West, and I am suggesting that the end of the ancient Christian misunderstanding of Jesus is now allowing him to emerge as its greatest early prophet. Like Nietzsche, he thought that the end of the old moral realism or objectivism was a major event, so much so that he sometimes spoke, it seems, as if one world was coming to an end and a new world was even now already coming into being. But I have already suggested that even the dim English can handle this line of talk, because in their use of the word 'Jerusalem' they already speak of a new and better world that is simultaneously a task for us – something that we must build – *and* a hidden present reality, *and also* a great supernatural future consummation for which we need to be prepared. William Blake was mad and talented enough to have similar ideas around the time of the French Revolution. So we have heard it all before. Even prosy old Matthew Arnold was 'a wanderer between two worlds / one dead, the other not yet ready to be born'.

The new moral anthropocentrism can still shock. The crucial event is that a human being has somehow been able to wrest control of the ethical from heaven and the eternal world, and give it to us. As Prometheus stole fire from the gods, and suffered a terrible punishment for it, so Jesus has somehow been able to seize and transmit to us the true nature of the ethical, and once humanity has grasped and fully appropriated something of what the ethical really is then, alas, it cannot be given back.

Romantic religious conservatives like J. R. R. Tolkien have dreamt that it might be possible to give back the fearsome gift that ought by rights never to have fallen into our hands. But it cannot be done. The new knowledge may be terrible; it may somehow be connected with the Twilight of the Gods, but we cannot lose it. It is indelible. Prometheus was punished for what he had done, and so was Jesus. For his *blasphemy*.

The first generation of Christians, around the years 33–55 or so CE, seem to have had little idea of why Jesus had been executed. In *The Gospel of Jesus* all that comes through as probably historical is that Jesus had sharply offended the Temple authorities, and had by them been arrested and handed over to Pilate for execution. One of his own group perhaps betrayed him. Nothing else: what we call 'the passion narrative' is a later fiction, with many layers, superimposed one above another as the early Christian community struggled – with, in the end, only partial success – to develop a theory of what had happened in the death of Jesus.

In the next generation belief in Jesus' resurrection had become common. People are beginning to think of him as still alive, the vindicated and exalted Messiah-designate who was waiting in the heavenly world for his moment to come. Their job was to stay cool and disciplined, and to wait vigilantly for his speedy return. Evidently a really major religious change is brewing, and gentile converts are beginning to seek admission to the infant Church. Should they be required to undergo circumcision, and to accept the Jewish Torah? Among Jesus' followers strong and first-hand oral tradition was well aware of his extremely radical attitude to the Torah, to the Temple, to the professional interpreters of the Torah, to tradition – in short, to the entire established religious and moral order. So it was perfectly possible for some to argue that the Torah was now annulled, and also for others to regard Jesus as having been a blasphemer, a 'sorcerer' who had tried to lead the Jewish people astray. This view of Jesus as a blasphemer is naturally enough reflected, not only in the passion narratives, but also in the Mishnah. Matthew, a relatively Judaizing evangelist, ascribes to Jesus statements denying outright the charge that he sought to destroy the Law, implying that Matthew must have had an audience willing to accept that Jesus had been an orthodox Jew, which is surprising.

For Jesus *was* a blasphemer, at least, by implication. Then, as now, blasphemy was originally an offence directly against God himself. But people are touchy, and will raise a hue and cry against someone who criticizes the established religious order, or who simply 'disrespects' their own religious feelings. Certainly, Jesus' ethical radicalism was such that it both led to his death, and also led to a very long-sustained struggle to produce a satisfactory *theory* of his death. At last, by the time of Luther, it was becoming possible to see in Jesus' death, the death of God.

9

Self-Awareness, Self-Criticism

Until the late eighteenth century in Britain the dominant literary form (and form of oratory) was the sermon and its close relative, the edifying religious tract. Then, quite suddenly, the novel took over, accompanied in its rise by some other and closely related forms, especially biography and narrative history. The changeover here was a change from an old world in which each individual's most important relationship was her inner relationship within her own conscience to the eternal God, or to the moral standard (Have I offended God? Am I still in a state of grace?) – a changeover, I say, to a new world in which each individual's most important relationships are her 'horizontal' relations with other human beings within the general flow of events in time in the human lifeworld.

What matters now in this new world is not how our heroine measures up when she is assessed *on her own* against a transcendent lawlike or lawgiving Standard, but whether she can be shrewd enough to retain her own innocence and charm intact as she negotiates her relations with other people during the difficult years of transition between the conclusion of her education and her marriage. The young male hero of a picaresque novel must rather similarly overcome a difficult beginning, launch himself into independent life at sea or in the city, and survive all the sudden ups and downs of fortune, until finally we see him securely established as a man among men in the world of men. Then perhaps he can think of finding himself a wife.

The novel quickly became a hugely popular medium, and

one in which women writers, heroines and readers were very prominent. But people are conservative, and for some generations many battled to retain the world-view of old-style theological morality within the world-view and the plotting of the novel. Could Anthony Trollope be permitted to publish a novel in which a fallen woman is rehabilitated, and even comes to a happy ending? Could Thomas Hardy get away with calling Tess *A Pure Woman*? But the novel is a profoundly secular and feminist medium, and however much fuss Victorian moralism might make it was bound to lose in the end. Today you will read dozens, perhaps hundreds of novels before you come across one that takes seriously the old 'theological' moral vocabulary of *sin* and *fallenness*, *conscience* and *the moral law*, *duty* and *obligation*. We are and have long been in a different world (although unfortunately a good deal of our professional academic study of Ethics and Christian Ethics does not seem yet to have noticed what has happened).

In this new world there are new moral requirements, for which we use a new vocabulary: life skills, emotional intelligence, empathy and the sort of shrewdness that Dr Samuel Johnson described as woman's 'natural advantages' – meaning, I suppose, her ability to *steer* a man in the desired direction without his being aware of being steered. These life skills and personal skills that are so important to people in the new only-human world – a world in which Elizabeth Bennett is queen – require a rather high degree of consciousness; and what is more, upon analysis it appears that critical self-awareness, and management of *other people's* precise degree of awareness of what's going on, is surprisingly many-stranded and complex, in a way of which the older Aristotle-to-Kant 'theological' types of moral theory knew nothing.

In Aristotle and everyone else for a very long time, all that matters when we are judging the morality of an act is the *intention* of the agent. In order to act fully responsibly, the moral agent needs to know the facts of the moral case, needs to know (and to recognize the authority of) the moral rule that bears upon the case, needs to be in a position to decide freely and without duress what he is to do, and must fully *intend* to do what he does. To put it really bluntly, in the traditional scheme of thought all I need in order to act rightly is to know right from wrong, and to know what I'm doing. That's it: one doesn't require any very high level of consciousness *at all*. It is enough to keep within the Law, and sincerely mean to do so.

The new morality depends very largely upon an elaborate play of levels of consciousness, very elegantly laid out in *Pride and Prejudice*. We know, it's obvious, that Elizabeth and Darcy are fated to marry, even though she thinks she detests him. For this to come about, Elizabeth must sort out her political relations with the other women who may claim to own a piece of Darcy, plus the relevant family members and friends: and there is also the odd loose cannon rolling about who may cause trouble, namely Wickham. In one way or another all the problems get sorted out. Darcy's young sister is befriended, Jane is allocated to the somewhat dull but cheerful Bingley, Charlotte (poor Charlotte!) gets the egregious Mr Collins, Lady Catherine de Burgh is demolished with overwhelming firepower, and Darcy himself conveniently restores himself to favour. Elizabeth's parents are not likely to object – would they *dare*? – and Lady Catherine's young daughter is of no account.

The final joke of the plot is, not merely that all these characters are so unaware of being moved around, but that Elizabeth herself does not really know at what point she changed her mind about Darcy and decided that she would have him. Questioned directly on the point, she jokes that the size and splendour of Darcy's house and grounds at Pemberley changed her feelings about him. But she probably does not know too clearly what's going on, even as she is expertly moving everyone into place.

In all this the traditional sexual and family ethics must be observed, of course, and so it is, to the letter: the novel is after all set in the last years of the old Anglican landowners' England, and we are only a generation away from the emergent feminism and paganism of Charlotte and Emily Brontë, and from Mrs Gaskell's Manchester. In Jane Austen's time the old religious, social and moral order is still in place, almost unquestioned. But it is fast becoming only part of the background, part of the joke, for Austen is writing high romantic comedy, and opening up a new moral world in which the play of different levels of consciousness and freedom in personal relationships has completely replaced the older sense of oneself as a moral being under God, and subject to his Law. In this new moral world the older vocabulary has been demythologized into life-skills, and talk about what you can and cannot 'get away' with, and about what is 'socially acceptable' or, on the contrary, 'totally unacceptable'. You have to be quick on the uptake and wide awake, or they'll 'run rings' round you.

Nor is all this an unnecessary digression. Not at all: for this play of levels of consciousness is after all something of a traditional Jewish speciality. The Jews have always excelled in the comedy of personal relationships, and secular prose fictions are prominent in both the Hebrew Bible and the Apocrypha. Nor are battling females exactly uncommon among the Jews, and anyone can enjoy the story of indignant Susannah's revenge upon the two old men who spied on her bathing. A very familiar example of a prophet telling a story in order to create moral self-awareness is Nathan's parable told to David in 2 Samuel 12. So it should not really be a surprise that in the core-tradition of Jesus' teaching there are several very striking examples. From Q and from *Thomas* we get the well-known:

> You see the sliver in your friend's eye, but don't see the timber in your own eye. When you take the timber out of your own eye, then you will see well enough to remove the sliver from your friend's eye.[15]

The scholars, the professional interpreters of the Law, are

so pleased with themselves that they cannot see the absurd-
ity of their own prayers: 'I thank you, God, that I am not
like everybody else . . .'[16] Nor do they find anything absurd
in their own enjoyment of dressing-up in special clothes and
being treated everywhere with special respect. But perhaps
the most striking of these examples is the story of the Friend
at Midnight, who comes knocking at the door asking for
three loaves so that he can entertain an unexpected guest.
Jesus sets up this situation in order to ask what makes the
central character get out of bed in order to do as he is asked.
He won't do it, says Jesus, just for friendship's sake: he does
it because he'd be ashamed not to.[17]

This is very remarkable indeed for its date, and I'd be
glad to hear of a parallel. Jesus recognizes, presumably with
approval, that one of the strongest of all motives for action is
our need to live up to our own ego-ideal – that is, my sense
of myself as a person who can be relied upon to live up to
certain moral standards. To function as a person, it seems,
I need to maintain *my own self-respect*, and this rules out
certain kinds of pretence, laziness, deceitfulness and so on
in my dealings with others. The 'ego-ideal' is of course a
Freudian invention; but it is also a very modern invention. It
implies a radical-humanist ethical theory, for it implies that
we ourselves invent and adopt for ourselves a certain, basic
pass-standard ethic that is, apparently, essential to our ability
to function as one person among others. In order to write the
story of my own life, I need to know and to stick to a story
about the kind of person I myself purport to be. *Through the
ego-ideal* each of us is *his or her own* hardest taskmaster,
and there is no need at all to suppose that 'moral experience'
demands a realist view of the moral standard.

At first glance, it seems barely credible that Jesus should be
so far ahead of his own time as that. But the Jews have always
been good at personal relations, and especially at psychology.
The so-called Court History of David is nowhere near as old
as many scholars still claim. It dates from probably only two
or three centuries before Jesus, but its ferocious psychologi-

cal insight still shocks. Try reading 2 Samuel 13, and check how you react when you get to verse 15.

Religious and cultural traditions can be curiously *dual*. Synagogue Judaism, new in Jesus' day and still around today, may seem to be the very model of a religion and ethic of revealed Divine Law. But the same tradition has *also*, all along, somehow been much more radical-humanist than any other in the world.

10

Performance Art

The early sayings-Gospels give very little biographical information about Jesus. Among the sayings that have some chance of being his own there is no information at all about himself, apart from the occasional use of a phrase equivalent to 'that's what I'm here for'. Otherwise he is completely lacking in self-concern. The historical Jesus simply cannot be imagined as making great 'claims' about his own status, just as he cannot really be pictured as ever quietly attending synagogue or Temple worship, melting unobtrusively into the group as if he were just another observant Jew of his time. Jesus is *never* unobtrusive. Even the Christian preacher's picture of him as 'a man of prayer' is wrong: there are nine references to Jesus at prayer in the canonical Gospels, of which six are found in Luke. Only a very few allusions to prayer make it into *The Gospel of Jesus*,[18] and if we were to tighten up the historicity-criteria only a little, almost nothing would remain.

In short, the Jesus of history appears to be completely given over to his moral teaching. We are not told anything about his life, nor about how he commonly spoke informally. The parables and epigrams were probably carefully composed and polished by him, and then taught to be learnt by heart by his followers. As for the conversation-pieces, we simply cannot judge whether any of them is traceable back to a memory of an actual occasion. In general, the likelihood is that the conversation has been invented by the tradition in order to provide a lead-in to the punchline by Jesus that ends the brief exchange. The reason for this last observation is that sometimes the setting contrived for the punchline is unconvincing and discordant. In which case, the punchline may still be a good recollection, but the conversational setting is no more than a somewhat-unintelligent contrivance of much later date.

In a number of cases, however, the sayings-tradition does seem to give us a few scraps of good information about Jesus' actions. Thus, in *The Gospel of Jesus* 16, five healings are collected together. All are from Mark, one being also independently attested by the *Egerton Gospel*. Four of these healings involve touch. It seems clear that Jesus did touch the sick, and that the significance of this symbolic action was the same for him as it is in many other traditions. In prescientific times, sickness was very often associated with uncleanness, madness and a state of complete social exclusion. The touch of a royal or other charismatic person was felt to be powerfully therapeutic, because it symbolized social acceptance and love. A vivid recent example is given by the famous photograph of Diana, Princess of Wales shaking hands with an AIDS victim. Against this background, it seems clear that Jesus' healings were symbolic actions of healing by welcoming back, and by reinstating the sick person. These actions had little to do with either medicine or miracles as *we* understand them: they expressed Jesus' *social* vision.

John Dominic Crossan has made this point clearly,[19] and has done so not only in the case of Jesus' healing touch, but also in Jesus' practice of welcoming all and sundry into the company of his followers, and even of being distinctly slack about ritual handwashing before his festive meals. A spot of 'pollution' does not worry him, because it is not of any real *ethical* importance.

There must be a question about how literally Jesus' reported feasting is to be taken. In Israel today one can see a cluster of ancient fishermen's stone huts at the ruins of Capernaum, and the excavated remains of major priestly houses near the Temple steps in Jerusalem. Each fisherman had one room, about 3 metres square, and the Sadducee had a dining room perhaps about 6 metres by 4 metres; so how could Jesus have held the sort of large and miscellaneous feast that the Gospels describe, and which Italian painters have depicted, within *any* private house? It looks like a physical impossibility.

Nevertheless, it seems beyond doubt that Jesus did attach great importance to table-fellowship, and that he used it in order to symbolize and to enact his own campaign against the separation of one human being from another by ritual and class barriers. The later Church used 'communion' and 'excommunication' in order not to include but to exclude, by drawing a very clear and sharp line between *us* and *them*, between insiders and outsiders, the included and the excluded, and so reminding us once again that the ethics of the Church is often the exact opposite of the ethics of Jesus.

One can see why, for class and other related barriers remain hugely powerful and mysterious even to this day – and not only in India, for ask yourself: Exactly when did you last invite a vagabond or other disreputable person to join you at table in your own house? Jesus' egalitarianism, his desire to see a fully reconciled, face-to-face society, remains today as far ahead of our actual practice as ever.

It is worth adding to this very short list of Jesus' symbolic actions his very bold readiness to include public women in his band of followers. Many people are unaware that in Jesus' time – and especially in Jerusalem – respectable married women lived in some degree of seclusion, much as they do in modern Islam. Widows with money to help support his group may have been among Jesus' followers, but otherwise women who wandered about in public risked a general assumption that they were more or less streetwalkers. Nevertheless, the tradition, both early and late, gives the impression that Jesus was quite unconcerned, and also that there was never any scandal – which is odd, because the Gospels are usually quick to report any hostile rumours. Even odder is the fact that although Jesus' ethical message was in general intensely concerned with human relationships – the clouds that hang over them, the barriers that obstruct them – he has almost nothing to say about sex. Perhaps the best comment we can make is that, although marriage was highly esteemed, sexual relationships *just as such* did not have the great interest and moral importance in those days that they do now. In his stories Jesus concentrates chiefly upon housewives and on the relation of master to man at work.

We may conclude this brief review of Jesus' symbolic actions with a comment on his relation to the Temple. Many scholars, perhaps most, think that the Temple authorities *were* instrumental in procuring the arrest of Jesus and his subsequent execution by the Romans. If so, he had presumably offended the Temple authorities in some way. But we don't know how. The two best-known stories, describing the cleansing of the Temple, and depicting him preaching against it on its steps, are both devised to show Jesus as fulfilling prophecies in the Hebrew Bible, and are therefore not historical. The earliest sayings-Gospels were compiled *before* the destruction of the Temple in the year 70, and therefore are not concerned with responding to that event. After the year 70 it became important to portray Jesus as having denounced the Temple and as having prophesied its destruction, so that stories saying as much were duly wheeled out. But the earliest evidence available to us leaves us quite unsure about whether it was indeed the Temple authorities who took the lead in bringing about his end, and if so, what Jesus may have done to offend them. My own guess is that at least some of Jesus' contemporaries grasped how revolutionary his ethical teaching was, and that it was *their* indignation that underlies the charge of 'blasphemy' and the belief that he had come to 'destroy' the Law. Of course, in thinking that avoidance-behaviour designed to preserve ritual purity was morally irrelevant, in being unimpressed by the Temple and the sacrificial system generally, and in using a kind of performance art to dramatize his message, Jesus was standing firmly in the tradition of prophets such as Jeremiah and Ezekiel. It is almost the only respect in which he can be thought of as a 'traditionalist'.

II

Justice and *Ressentiment*

Ever since the first rise of synagogue Judaism it has been possible to see individual Jews as arranged along a spectrum from the most intensely sociable to the most intensely 'withdrawn', bookish and mystical. At the sociable end of the spectrum, Jewish culture is notable for its thoroughgoing humanism, its interest in domestic life, in comedy and in storytelling, and (especially in America) for its novelists. For people at this end of the spectrum, the 'horizontal' ethical relationship to one's fellow human being is the most important thing in one's life.

At the opposite end of the scale are those – almost always males – who spend long days in the study-house, reading the Jewish law-books and other sacred texts and the many commentaries upon them. The scholars are mystically inclined, and they spend as much of their time as they can poring in solitude over texts that link them to the world of the Sacred. These are the ultra-orthodox, the pious, the Hasidim. They are conscientious husbands, but their real interest is in the 'vertical' relationship to God mediated, for them, by Jewish writings.

Neither of these two groups would deny for a moment that people in the other group are authentically Jewish. The Hasidim do not usually accuse the sociables of 'atheism', and the sociables do not customarily accuse the ultra-orthodox of being crazies. On the whole, the two groups feel that however irritating they find each other, they are all Jews and must tolerate each other. But they are of course profoundly different in world-view.

Now to which of the two groups did Jesus belong? Obviously, to the sociables: his contemporaries complained loudly that he was an extreme sociable, who caroused with gluttons and drunks.[20] Almost the whole content of his teaching, both the parables and the epigrammatic sayings, is set in a secular-humanist world, with only the most minimal supernatural apparatus. Considering that he is supposed to be the founder of the greatest and most influential of the world's religions, it is a shock to realize that Jesus has no teaching about 'spirituality'. By that I mean that among his teachings there is virtually nothing that presupposes the absolute primacy of the individual's inner and secret relation to God, and that prescribes ways of purifying ourselves and getting closer to God. It's true that Jesus has the well-loved and beautiful sayings about not letting ourselves fall a prey to undue anxiety.[21] But the bald fact is that he does not teach any system of stages on one's journey into God. There is no account of the contemplative life, nor any *Itinerarium mentis ad Deum* ('Itinerary of the mind on its way to God', the title of a book by Bellarmine). From the classical Latin and Greek Christian standpoint, Jesus has to be judged a most unspiritual man. Later Christian spirituality was always Platonic, and Jesus was no Platonist. His overriding interest is in the space between one human being and another, and in the manifold ways in which that space can be blocked or clouded by an utterly amazing range of 'reactive' or 'negative' emotions and conventional barriers.

Nietzsche sums up the whole range of reactive or negative emotions in the single French word *ressentiment* (reactive feeling), a word that, for want of any better, we English speakers have also had to adopt. They include, for example, wariness, suspicion, doubt, hesitation, mistrust, touchiness, scorn, disgust, dislike, envy, lust, disapproval, repugnance, contempt, impatience, malice, irritation, anger, rage, fury, fear, terror, hatred, boredom, indifference, recoiling, seething resentment, begrudging, outrage, indignation at, despair of, and many, many more. I think I could easily run up to 50 or 60. It really is astonishing that such a very large range of negative emotional reactions to another person can and do surge up in us, and make us all desire to put as much distance as possible between that person and ourselves.

What about the 'positive' emotions? They do not cloud or block our relation to the other person. They are on the whole very cool and 'transparent', and unexpectedly few in number: regard, attention, interest, sympathy, pity, respect, admiration, allegiance, friendship and love. Of these only love is hot and therefore in danger both of 'blinding' the lover, and also perhaps of provoking a negative emotion in the other who is displeased to find herself its object.

In general, the positive emotions as such present no particular moral problem. The ethically important issue, for a teacher such as Jesus, is the astoundingly large number and the violence of the negative or reactive emotions. They are in all ages the great threat to social peace. What's to be done about them? Why cannot people just get along with each other?

Nicos Kazantzakis has declared that there have been three great moral teachers of humankind: the Buddha, Jesus and Nietzsche. What did they have in common? All of them wished for a life without *ressentiment*. How could we reach this happy state? The Buddha seeks by the practice of meditation so to calm the passions that we simply do not suffer from *ressentiment*. On the basis of my knowledge of a few remarkable Buddhists, I believe his method can work. Nietzsche pursues an aristocratic ideal: one should be so disciplined, confident, sure of one's values, and magnanimous ('great-souled') that one simply does not *notice* injuries. Such a person is not touchy, nor quick to take offence. True magnanimity 'proofs' one's psychology against *ressentiment*, but I fear that it is very uncommon.

Jesus' answer is different again. It has the advantage of not requiring us either to do without the greatest of the *positive* emotions, human love, in the Buddha's manner, or to be aristocrats in Nietzsche's style. Instead, Jesus offers an interpretation of what he regards as the destructive core of all the very worst negative emotions. According to him, it is a seething sense of injustice and a desire for vengeance. At least in the Anglo-Saxon world, we know too well that many ordinary people will campaign relentlessly for decades in order to get what they describe as 'justice' – that is, retribution – on behalf either of themselves or of a very seriously wronged relative. The quest for 'justice' has become an avenging Fury driving them on and (as they understand very clearly) for them there can be no 'closure' until it is sated. Till then, they cannot and will not give up the hunt.

Justice? It is vengeance, it is getting even, it is retaliation, it is payback, it is fair shares, it is equity. It is a vendetta: it can go on and on, back and forth in a cycle of violence. Jesus' remedy, in a surprising number of his major parables and sayings, is to launch a remarkable and disturbing satirical attack upon the ordinary person's desire for, and indeed *concept of*, justice.[22] We are intended to see the wrongness, the mean-spiritedness of the elder brother in the parable of the Prodigal Son, and of the day-labourers in the parable of the Vineyard who have put in the full day's work that they agreed upon that very morning. These characters, and others like them in Jesus' teaching, are too mean-spirited ever to be pleased by someone else's unmerited good fortune. They actually think that the good fortune of that other is tantamount to *an injustice to themselves*, despite the fact that (as the story makes clear) they will in any case still be getting exactly what they initially bargained for.

In short, as we found earlier, Jesus' view is that *ressentiment* is so strong, irrational and easily displaced that we cannot hope to check its poisonous destructive effects by an ethic of law and strict justice alone. A touch of pure 'grace' or gratuitous generosity of spirit is needed. Without it, human beings are lost and will stay lost. In our own world the point is very familiar to negotiators who are struggling to make peace between two communities who have been bitterly hostile to each other for centuries. Each community clings tenaciously to its own story of cherished grievances, justified retaliation and so on. To make peace, you must persuade many people who have bad memories to be almost supernaturally 'big' and generous, and you must go *beyond justice*. It's a lot to ask, but it has to be done. Without that touch of supererogatory, 'absurd' love nothing can be done to make peace between hostile communities.

On this point, the great originality and power of Jesus as a moral teacher has been recognized around the world by many people who have no liking at all for Christianity. But there is another interesting twist to his argument in a Q saying as follows:

God causes the sun to rise on both the bad and the good, and sends rain on both the just and the unjust. As you know, God is generous to the ungrateful and the wicked.[23]

Both Matthew and Luke place this saying close to their version of the saying about loving your enemies. Jesus says that it is no great moral achievement to return the love of someone who loves you: even sinners do that. What he insists upon is the moral necessity of showing gratuitous, unmerited, excessive love if we are to break the chain of *ressentiment*, rebounding back and forth and spreading. But Jesus tries to strengthen his own argument by saying that, at the cosmic level, God *too* treats the undeserving with unmerited generosity, for the rain that every Middle Eastern peasant longs to see falls equally upon the just and the unjust.[24]

Here Jesus slips up badly in his philosophy of religion. If the situation is that the way things go is just the same for everyone, and is *not* tilted to ensure that the good guys do well and the bad guys get thumped, the obvious inference is surely that there is no moral Providence whatever at work in human life. How on earth can Jesus argue that the world's manifest indifference and neutrality is best interpreted as evidence of God's wonderful love for sinners?

Perhaps we have to understand the saying against the background of the older belief that is expressed very clearly in a line in the Psalms: 'I have been young and now am old: yet saw I never the righteous forsaken nor his seed begging their bread.'[25] The 'Deuteronomic' school of writers, who produced the books of Deuteronomy and the Former Prophets in the Hebrew Bible, asserted the traditional popular belief that in the long run 'Honesty is the best policy', and 'Your sins will find you out', 'Your chickens will come home to roost' – and so on, and on. The righteous walk on a narrow way that leads to life, and sinners are walking along an easy broad way that leads to destruction – a saying attributed by Matthew to Jesus himself! *The Gospel of Jesus* accepts only

> Jesus would say, 'Struggle to get in through the narrow door; I'm telling you, many will try to get in, but won't be able.'[26]

This version of the saying is from Q/Luke: Matthew has expanded it to incorporate the traditional contrast, found in Deuteronomy, between the Way of Life and the Way of Death, and by so doing has made Jesus simply contradict himself, because it is in the same 'Sermon on the Mount' that Jesus has already committed himself to the much more intelligent view that the way things go does *not* discriminate so as regularly to provide a happy ending for the good people, and personal ruin for the bad people. Interestingly, even St John's Gospel similarly makes Jesus talk sense for once, in its discussion of the man born blind (a point on which Luke adds a further comment from Jesus about the falling of the Tower of Siloam).[27] If even John could get Jesus right on this point, why couldn't Matthew do the same?

Thus widening the discussion, however, leaves us as far as ever from the solution to our initial question: how on earth can Jesus suggest that the falling of the rain and the shining of the sun upon a wicked farmer's field is somehow evidence of the overflowing generosity of God towards the wicked? Is he not attempting an impossible *tour de force*? The best answer I can give for the present is that Jesus lived in a society in which everyone believed in a Moral Providence, and the Nietzschean view, that 'there is no moral world-order', because the way things go is morally strictly neutral, simply could not be seriously considered, just as in today's America politicians have to appear to be devout Christians, and Hollywood films have to have happy – i.e. 'moral' – endings. It was in the one case, and is in the other, a matter of culture, and of what professions and beliefs happen to be socially *compulsory* at a particular time and place.

As for Jesus, if he was not a foundationalist seeking to give a cosmic backing to his ethical teaching, then I suggest that he was recommending an attitude. Many people in the Jewish tradition (like the author of Psalm 73) were provoked to despair and anger by the prosperity of the wicked. Jesus says: 'Don't let yourself be provoked into *ressentiment* by the prosperity of the wicked. Instead, be magnanimous, and teach yourself to see in it the grace of God, giving them time to repent. Too many people who have seen the blood of the innocent crying out for vengeance have allowed themselves to develop the revolting belief in a sadistic and vengeful God.' To this day we hear such people say: 'I hope he rots in Hell.' Don't ever let yourself get to be like that.

This interpretation at least has the advantage of being consistent with the best of Jesus' own ethical teaching. But of course it still leaves us with the question of Jesus' own philosophy of religion. Was he a non-realistic theist? Should we perhaps see him as (like the great Egyptian novelist Naguib Mahfouz) battling not against God, but against a certain human *idea* of God? What view of God does his teaching suggest?

12

The Blasphemer, Reconsidered

The gods have long – and no doubt with good reason – feared that human technology might one day present a serious threat to them. In the Old Testament, God (here expressedly named as Yahweh/Jehovah) is made very uneasy by the sight of the first skyscraper, the Tower of Babel, and takes action to confuse and scatter its builders.[28] In Greece Zeus was similarly rattled by the thought of what humans might be able to do with fire, and he hid it. But the Titan Prometheus managed to steal fire from heaven and bring it back down to earth for humankind to use. Zeus seems to have recognized that the blow to his own power when humans began efficiently to harness and exploit the power of fire was irreversible, but he could at least inflict an exemplary public punishment upon Prometheus. And so he did: it was a horrible punishment, an agony renewed every day.

Our argument so far can be read as hinting that the ethical teaching of Jesus could be interpreted as committing the sin of Prometheus, but on a far, far grander scale. For in Jesus' teaching sovereignty over the entire moral realm is being quietly removed from heaven, and relocated within the human heart. He redeems humankind by liberating us from heteronomy – moral government by a law or standard quite independent of ourselves and imposed upon us by another. Moral realism is a form of servitude or slavery, and people who have escaped from it and have learnt to enjoy freedom cannot possibly wish to go back to servanthood.

Even now, however, it remains true that a great many human beings still enjoy the objectivity and the security of living within a great institution, fixed, readymade, and with its own built-in rules of behaviour. To them, pure moral autonomy is terrifying: they don't want that degree of freedom, and might well be angry at the immorality, or even the *blasphemy*, of someone who offers it to them, seeing him as advocating a condition of complete indiscipline and anarchy.

How far was Jesus, in his own eyes or in the eyes of some of his contemporaries, talking in a way that risked, or courted, or even justified such accusations?

In the earliest sayings-traditions available to us – Q, *Thomas* and others, as selectively reported in *The Gospel of Jesus* – there are already traces of much grumbling about Jesus and his message. He's mad, say his relatives. He can cast out devils only because he is himself in league with the devil, say others, perhaps because he used his own forceful and charismatic personality to shock people who were having convulsions, and so bring them abruptly to their senses. The strictly religious protest loudly about his moral laxity, about the company he keeps, about the washing of hands before meals, and about the Sabbath. Others found his feasting oddly in contrast with the fasting of John's disciples.

The word 'blasphemy' is used only once,[29] on the occasion when Jesus has been heard to promise the forgiveness of his sins to the paralytic at Capernaum. But the text here is controversial, and I think it comes from a much later period, when believers have begun to ascribe something approaching divine status and powers to the *person*, rather than to the words, of Jesus.

Otherwise, the charge of blasphemy was unknown to the early tradition. All we have to go on is a few hints that have already been introduced into this discussion. The most important are these: first, Matthew would not portray Jesus as saying, 'Don't imagine that I have come to annul the Law and the Prophets',[30] unless that were in many people's eyes the obvious implication of his teaching. And after all, the early Church, unlike the Synagogue, did indeed decide *not* to impose the Torah upon Gentile converts. Second, there are the sayings in which Jesus exhibits a very lax attitude to the Law, such as the famous one uttered in the cornfield on the Sabbath, where Jesus ranks the human being as higher in status than the Law itself. Its role is only instrumental: we may bend it if we so wish. In his version of the story of the paralytic at Capernaum Matthew similarly has the crowd praising God for 'giving such authority to men'.[31] The hint here is that the teaching of Jesus implies the end of the rule of religious law, and the arrival of a kind of human being who is more radically free and autonomous than ever before; and it is a hint that perhaps began to emerge very early in the development of the sayings-tradition.

The third and last of these hints that may account both for Jesus' popular appeal and for the growing suspicion and anger of the authorities is his attack, already discussed, upon the moral adequacy of *any* objective moral code that purports, by setting up a system of reciprocal rights and duties, to create a peaceful and just society. On the contrary Jesus, from the first it seems, followed the great prophets in believing that instead of looking to a written law-code to create the good society, we must look for a transformation of the human *heart*. The law will be written on people's hearts: God will take away their hearts of stone and give them instead hearts of flesh.[32] I have taken this to mean that Jesus is radicalizing the teaching of Jeremiah and Ezekiel, and going anthropocentric and emotivist. This is an extraordinary change: Jesus is *secularizing* ethics, *historicizing* it, *humanizing* it. And perhaps Jesus himself, some of his audience, and some of his enemies, got just a whiff of this early on. But in that cultural setting, where the ideas of God and of living by a code of revealed Divine Law were so closely linked, to question the Law was, by implication, to question God.

Not, however, *consciously*. In some forty years of writing I have several times found myself taking ten years or more to understand my own new ideas. When we have a quite new idea, it is rough and ill-fitting. One has to keep turning it over in one's mind. Only after several years does it get rubbed smooth, so that it can run smoothly and mesh in with the rest of our thinking; and only then do we begin to trace out its full implications. It is for reasons of this kind that the full implications of Darwinism for our culture are still not completely traced out, even after 150 years.

In the case of Jesus, the new idea is even bigger. It is the idea that the entire history of the human race reflects a long, slow transition from heterologous to autologous thinking and living. At first, human beings were too weak, confused and fearful to be able to think their own situation in life in any sort of head-on way. It was too terrifying for them. They had to start from a point outside and above themselves, and to think almost everything in an objectifying, roundabout, symbolic way. It was less painful to think in this heterologi-cal and magico-religious way: we much preferred to think *about ourselves indirectly*, by thinking about a spirit-world whose denizens *did* have knowledge of and control over our world, and knew how we should live. God's power and immortality was a much pleasanter topic than my own weak-ness and mortality. So the earlier part of the human story was a long attempt to do theology – celebrating the world of the gods and other spirits, working out their organization and their power-relations, their social life, their knowledge of and control over events, and their moral power; and all this in the long-term hope that as we celebrate them and strive to please them, then gradually, gradually, more and more of what they are will rub off upon us. The gods represent to us what we hope we can become.

In the earlier 'theological' period the spirit-world gradu-ally becomes totalized in a Bronze-Age society of gods liv-ing in places like Mount Olympus, and including within the celestial 'cabinet' specialists in law-giving, in war, in agri-culture, in technology and so on. Then polytheism evolves into monotheism, as our picture of the unity of the world and therefore of the divine knowledge of and control over the world becomes clearer and more systematic. But the One God of ethical monotheism is at first too violent and capricious, and ethical monotheism next develops into *nomothetic monotheism*, in which God's action has become so regular and rational that he is in effect quite hidden behind the systems of law, natural and revealed, through which alone he manifests himself and orders everything.

At this point of maximal theological development (prophetic monotheism, Islam) the long slow withdrawal of God, and his progressive handover of all his powers, attributes, and spheres of interest to us, is already under way. God is beginning to seem hidden. This is partly because as our vision of the world becomes completely law-governed we have less and less need, or even ability, to glimpse or to infer the supposed Lawgiver working behind the scenes: but also because the handover from God to humans began right at the very beginning, at the moment when human life first began. Thus God gives to Adam a little of his own power by giving him first Woman – and therewith, society, offspring, descendants, a human social world – and then the right to name animals – and therewith the power, not only to find and hunt them, but also to *domesticate* the beasts and so make the transition to settled life.

In this whole long process of handover, the single greatest step was the transfer from God to humans of sovereignty over the moral realm – and therewith, the power of pure morality and freedom, the power to understand and accept that we ourselves are the only makers and the continual re-negotiators of our own moral world, of our own values and of everything that makes our lives worth living. When we fully understand all this, we are thinking autologously, and *from the heart*. We have arrived: we have come to ourselves. Genesis already knows that this knowledge is the greatest knowledge of all, but the Yahweh of Genesis is still a bit jealous of us, and reluctant to bear the thought of handing it all over yet awhile.[33] But finally in the ethical teaching of Jesus we do glimpse – a little more clearly than in any other ancient teacher's work – the greatest handover finally beginning to take place. The principle of morality, of moral sovereignty and creativity, comes down from heaven and relocates itself within the human heart. Ethics ceases to be something One, commanding and out-there, and becomes instead something purely human, subjective and emotive. We learn at last to trust ourselves, and the feelings that flow out of our own hearts.

So God comes down from heaven and dies to make us free, and the final revelation of God is the Kingdom of God and the disappearance of God, as God vanishes into our hearts. But at first it was all much too big to be thought out and voiced consciously, and you could say that the whole history of ecclesiastical Christianity, roughly from the years 50 to 1830, was a period in which people very slowly digested what had happened. One can see the process of digestion happening in the history of Western painting, or by setting up a little series like Jesus → Blake → Nietzsche, Blake being just about midway between Jesus and Nietzsche. The further development of human consciousness after Nietzsche is perhaps only just now stirring, since the 1960s.

Christianity, then, was an interim formation to help us through the period during which we have been slowly coming to ourselves. Perhaps unavoidably, it did involve a good deal of remythicization and a severe distortion of Jesus, as the full meaning of his message was deferred for some 18 centuries.

The very early community at first preserved only the teaching of Jesus, to which clung only the tiniest fragments of information about his life. It was known that he had died a shameful public death, and it was known that Mary of Magdala claimed to have had a vision or apparition of him soon after his death. But phantasms of the recently dead have always been common, and are still very common even to this day, so nobody really thought of theologizing about Mary's report for many years, until, somewhere around the year 50 or so, a number of lines of thought and feeling perhaps converged. Thinking as they did, the earliest community believed that they encountered something of Jesus' own charisma and presence in hearing his words, and they also felt they met

him when they were in the company of those who had known
him and bore the tradition of his living word. There was in
addition the sense of his continuing presence at their com-
memorative meals, the testimony of Mary of Magdala, and
the effects of their searching of the Hebrew Scriptures for
'evidences' that might assist them in their attempts to understand the meaning of Jesus' unjust death.

It seems to have been in Peter and James, and especially in the contest between them for leadership of the young
community at Jerusalem, that the theology began to come
together. They testified that they had come to understand
that Jesus was risen, was exalted to heaven, was the Messiah-
designate, and would return to establish on earth the Kingdom he had preached. By the late 40s Paul, the self-confessed
latecomer, had arrived upon the scene, and soon he was rapidly developing the new theology in his letters to his small
communities of converts in various Gentile cities around the
eastern Mediterranean.

The whole new theology rested upon an intellectual mistake, the mistake that Jacques Derrida spent so much effort
upon demonstrating, of supposing that a person's own spoken
words, live or reported, can be 'animated' by the presence and
the intention of the speaker. But this mistake made it easy to
transfer the focus of interest from Jesus' words to his person,
and from ethics in this world to the heavenly world where
Jesus now was. In expressions like 'the Law of Christ' heteronomy was reinstated, and the apostles and their successors,
as inheritors of the authority of Jesus himself, became an
elite ruling group within the Church. In short, the developing
Church was, intellectually, a sad comedown from what the
historical Jesus had taught. But there it was: in the slightly
coarse language of British politics, Jesus had been 'kicked
upstairs', ennobled, promoted into the obscurity of the Upper
House, where he could do no further harm here below.

But the Church did not completely forget the words that
had set the whole process in motion. They survived, embedded in a thick overgrowth of later material, just as a trace

of the faith's original purely ethical and secular orientation lingered in the Lord's Prayer and the common Meal. In
the Enlightenment, Western culture grew more confident.
Knowledge grew, technology developed, and human attention turned at last back to this world. The supernatural word
faded, and morality after 1700 rapidly became more humanistic and indeed humanitarian. After a detour of 17 or 18
centuries, the world slowly began to become more Christian
at last. There began a great quest for the historical Jesus and
his original message that, despite a number of major setbacks,
has gradually made some progress.

We have made a considerable detour ourselves, and must
now ask: how far could either Jesus himself, or his original hearers, have been conscious of the implications of his
words, and of the mighty historical process that they were
setting in motion? Could they have grasped enough of what
he was about to explain why some of them thought of him as
a blasphemer?

No. If we had been there, and had said to them: 'The
dream of the Kingdom of God is the dream of a world in
which human beings have new hearts, and therefore have no
need of any external Lawgiver. They've grown up, they have
graduated from schooldays to adulthood, from milk to meat,
from tutelage to freedom. They have become ready to live
from the heart. Jesus – the *original* Jesus – on the evidence
of the surviving sayings attributed to him was a much more
radical figure than we have realized. The Christ of faith is
Jesus tamed, domesticated, and diminished by being tied
back into a relaunch of the old kind of religion. But we can
now see that there is a straight line from Jesus to Blake and
Dostoyevsky and Nietzsche . . .' and so on. If we'd said all
this, they'd have looked blank. All we can say with confidence is that the words of the original Jesus had considerable historical momentum. They tended, in the very long
run, to bring about the sort of changes and the sort of world
that they originally envisaged. And, contingently, only contingently, that is what has happened, and is still happening.

With our hindsight, there is a straight line from the teaching of Jesus to the Death of God; but they did not have any foresight that could correspond with our hindsight, and I don't think the historical Jesus could accurately be described as a blasphemer. All I will say for the present is that the original words of Jesus were what they are, and have in the long run produced the consequences that you now see around you.

13

Just How Secular?

It is important not to allow oneself to be sidetracked by questions of historicity, but in general I have been working with the hypothesis that we can know very little about the life or the personality of Jesus, but that we can say something with some confidence about his teaching.

Suppose then that we collect together the earliest, best-attested, and most likely-sounding traditions of Jesus' words that have reached us, and find that in them we can hear a very distinctive, coherent and vigorous 'voice', then it seems reasonable to suppose that this is likely to be an after-echo of the voice of Jesus himself. The Jesus Seminar (as we noted earlier) considered 1,330 reported sayings of Jesus. Of these 1,330, the Seminar's final report put 29 in the top grade and 184 in the second grade. The remainder, graded 'grey' and 'black', were judged to have little or no historical value. The highest poll figures of all were scored by a number of very familiar phrases, known to all as being of the 'Sermon-on-the-Mount' type. They were: 'turn the other cheek', 'when sued for your coat, give your cloak too', 'blessed are the poor', 'go the second mile', and 'love your enemies'.[34]

So in a sense the Seminar reached a rather conservative conclusion, because ordinary folk have long supposed that these sayings are typical of the teaching of Jesus. The Seminar decided that the common view is not far wrong. But what about the life and personality of Jesus? Paul's writing (at least when he is on his best form) does sometimes echo Jesus' values, and he does sometimes mention the tradition of 'words of the Lord'. But he evidently doesn't know a thing about the life and personality of Jesus, and he does not give any sign of regretting his ignorance. He is interested solely in the exalted, supernatural Jesus Christ who is now enthroned in heaven.

So conspicuous is Paul's lack of interest in the earthly Jesus that it has sometimes been suggested that the Synoptic Gospels were all produced by Jewish-Christian groups who wanted to register a protest, and to assert that on the contrary it was very important *not* to lose all memory of the Lord's earthly life. This suggestion is next easily coupled with another, namely that Mark, Matthew and Luke had a strong interest in making their accounts as accurate and reliable as possible, and therefore spent much labour in collecting whatever traditions they could get, whether written or oral.

That I cannot accept. The Synoptic Gospels as we have them follow in some detail the standard pattern for the life of a great holy man in antiquity;[35] the individual stories they contain have in very many cases evidently been worked up from Old Testament sources; and, third, in the details of their telling all or most stories evidently relate to the problems and needs of the early Christian groups for which they were written. The Gospels, to put it bluntly, were written at least partly to supply a lectionary of 'Gospels' – passages to be read and preached about at the Eucharist.

I conclude that the Gospel writers did preserve some good traditions of Jesus' *words*, but that they tell us almost nothing of historical value about Jesus' life and personality. To demonstrate the point, take another look at *The Gospel of Jesus* and in particular at the gulf between the dismally preachy and inspirational temptation-narrative in 1.20–31, and the direct and forceful voice of Jesus himself, as it emerges in the course of chapter 2.[36] The comparison makes it clear that the teachings, having been carefully designed for transmission, come through relatively well whereas the life is edifying fiction.

So: only the words are to be trusted, and it is with reference to them that I now pose the awkward question of just how secular a figure Jesus was.

At first sight, the teachings are startlingly secular, and their interest is purely ethical. The phrase 'the Kingdom of God' (or 'God's reign', or 'God's imperial rule') is not supported or filled out by any other doctrinal teaching about God, and I have suggested that, like 'Jerusalem' in modern left-wing English, it simply denoted 'the good society that we all long to see: the Dream'.

Otherwise, Jesus' supernatural apparatus is much thinner than (say) Shakespeare's. He shares the belief of his time in evil spirits, and like many another wandering teacher performs what – for want of any science-based medical theory – were then seen as healings. But his ordinary world-view, as revealed in the stories, is secular. His reported teaching does *not* presuppose a full acceptance of contemporary synagogue Judaism's beliefs, institutions and practices, as some like to claim:[37] on the contrary, when he refers to the Law, or to tradition, or to the professional interpreters and teachers of the Law, and when he appears at a synagogue or in the Temple, it is always and only as a critic and a revisionist. For him, it seems, nothing is sacred: indeed, I do not find in the core teaching anything to indicate that the classic distinctions, between the sacred and the secular realms, or between the clean and the unclean, figured in his world-view.

The most obvious theological comment on all this is that 'the Kingdom of God' in Jewish thought was an ideal future world in which the classical distinctions and contrasts of traditional religion have been erased. Jesus may have been deliberately *anticipating* (in the literal sense of seizing in advance, and acting out) such a world.[38] He is acting out the fulfilment of the traditional prophetic Dream, and to people whose thinking remains completely meshed into the old world-view of mediated religion he must appear completely secular.[39]

I think that is probably true. But the cast of mind revealed in Jesus' reversal-sayings is one that we usually regard as very far removed from any psychology that we could call 'religious'. Here I am thinking of his many sayings in *antithetical parallelism* that satirize and reverse conventional values. The writings of figures like Oscar Wilde and Bernard Shaw are full of such sayings – perhaps because these two wits were strongly influenced by Jesus.

For example, in a highly developed class society such as that established in England between 1880 and 1914 it was very common to hear upper-class persons deploring the alcohol consumption and the indolence of the working classes. It did not take any very deep thought to grasp that these leisured-class complainers displayed exactly the same vices themselves, in spades. Wilde makes the moral point very memorably by means of the carefully constructed witticism: 'Work is the curse of the drinking classes.' When people remarked: 'I wish I'd said that', Wilde would reply airily: 'You will, you will.' Why? Because Wilde's witticism was expressly *designed* to be remembered, transmitted and repeated.

Jesus' witticisms, such as the one where he says that when we have taken the log out of our own eye, we will be able to see better to remove the splinter from our friend's eye, have much the same structure, and make much the same moral point, as Wilde's. The only notable difference is that Jesus uses comic hyperbole, or wild exaggeration, in making his contrasts between the splinter and the log, the camel and the needle's eye, and so on. This was then, and is now, a popular taste, whereas Shaw and Wilde were using humour to get under the guard of their victims, the members of a West End theatre audience enjoying a night out in evening dress.

Now, to return to Jesus, his use of moral satire as a method of instruction surely indicates a cast of mind very different from what is normally regarded as 'religious', and it confirms the impression that Jesus was a notably secular moral teacher.[40] He had his eye upon the traditional 'Dream' of a better world to come – not above, but on this earth – but he sees the way to it as involving severe criticism of what currently passes for orthodox religion and conventional social morality. He has of course no thought of establishing a new religion. Rather, he follows the prophets: he has in mind a new trans-religious state of humanity, in which all the old ways of religious world-building will be fulfilled and therefore will disappear.

Finally, it is notable that Jesus is in this respect more secular than some (or even perhaps *all*) of his prophetic predecessors. The prophets usually claim that in the coming Dream-world Jerusalem will be rebuilt and full of people, the Jews will shine like lights, and the Gentiles will be queuing up to ask their advice – all of which means that the fulfilment of the Dream will *confirm* the Jew/Gentile distinction and vindicate Israel's religious faith. Jesus, however, is not ethnocentric. For him the Jew/Gentile distinction, and together with it the whole of positive or revealed religion, disappears in the Reign of God. And insofar as Jesus' own life and teaching is an anticipatory enactment of the Reign of God, it must appear to be, and is, completely secular.

It is not easy for most people to grasp that the most complete realization of Jesus' Dream is simply a universal secular humanism. But that is how it is. The Latin Church subsequently made itself cosmic, with its talk of dogmatic immutability, and of the Church Militant, Expectant and Triumphant; but this was an absurd misunderstanding of Jesus. His kingdom-sayings and parables could not be further from endorsing any crudely ethnocentric or sectarian world-view.

14

The God of Jesus

Speculative atheism was not common in antiquity. Travellers, as they went from city to city, were of course struck by the number and variety of the gods who were worshipped in this place and that. But if you saw the images of a god, his temple, the priesthood that served him, the daily rites they performed, and the people whose god he was, then, surely, the reality of the god was evident – or at least, there would be little sense or point in denying it.

In that social context, if you wished to campaign on behalf of your god, you did not usually say: 'My god exists, and your god does not exist.' You usually argued that your god was powerful, whereas the other person's god was weak and *unavailing* – not of much help in time of trouble.

What was Jesus' view? Given the cultural context within which he lived, he cannot be thought of as an 'atheist', a word that normally presupposes an interest in dogmatic metaphysical philosophy. Jesus did not think in those terms at all. It would be better to say that his interest is overwhelmingly *social* and not 'mystical' or dogmatic. He is *very* interested in the ethics of human interpersonal relationships, and scarcely at all in the 'vertical' relation of the individual self to God. He alludes to it here and there,[41] but he doesn't spend time on exploring it.

What about the counter-arguments? I have argued that the phrase 'the Kingdom of God', so much used by Jesus, is used by him rather as we might use the term 'Jerusalem', to describe a human world in which people live without *ressentiment*, and are completely *easy* with each other. The phrase 'the Kingdom of God', then, does not tell us anything about God, except that it stands for a world in which God has disappeared into human hearts, a human social world in which we are all of us in fully open communication – indeed, communion – with each other.

What of 'the Lord's Prayer'? Few modern Gospel critics think that *as a whole* it goes back to Jesus. It is something that was devised to be taught to new members of the early Church; but it may contain a few phrases of Jesus' own, drawn from the sayings-tradition.[42]

What about the God who, in Jesus' sayings about anxiety, looks after flowers and birds? Will he not, all the more, look after *you*?[43] This saying does not add to Jesus' supposed 'doctrine of God'. On the contrary, the whole passage argues that if the world of nature can look dazzlingly beautiful and can put on such a brave show despite being utterly ephemeral, well, you ought to be brave enough to do the same. The bird lives and sings without anxiety: why can't you do the same? The whole argument is making the case for being solar about life while we have it, and *not* for turning away from the world of life and looking instead for consolation to One who lives in a timeless and completely secure Better World outside life.

Finally, there is the word 'Abba'. Many critics argue that Jesus did actually pray, and used the word 'Abba' in speaking to God – which, it is suggested, indicates that he really *did* believe in God strongly and vividly. But this argument seems to equate authentic, high-grade religious conviction with the most naive anthropomorphism.[44] Unless the use of the word 'God' is tied in by strong intellectual ties to the structures of a rationally worked-out general world-view it is empty, and Freud's unkind verdict, 'He really *is* the believer's own father' – that is, a fantasy – is highly plausible. Here I recall that Jesus requires solar people, people who live expressively 'from the heart', *not* to be soft in the head, but to be streetwise, shrewd and sceptical. He does *not* for a moment advocate 'simple faith'.

From this short discussion I conclude that all the traditional preaching about Jesus as an exemplary man of prayer, motivated by a vivid and intimate faith in God, and, in short, as a standard Western-type popular theist, is wrong. But Jesus was no dogmatic atheist: few were, in his world. But we should look at the main uses of the *word* 'God' in his teaching as a whole, and of course what we find is that in the core tradition nine-tenths of all the uses of the word 'God' are in the phrase 'the Kingdom of God', a world in which God has come down from heaven and has disappeared into the flowing world of human personal relationships. Life without *ressentiment*, the life of love, life as we all guess it should be – that is the Reign of God. So the God of Jesus is God fully demythologized. Jesus *does* 'believe in God', but not as a wish-fulfilment: Jesus' God is the clear sweet moral atmosphere of the future world that Jesus speaks about, a world near to him and arriving in his activities and his teaching, but a world that is still somewhat ahead of us.

15

The Ambivalence of Jesus

Aristotle was the first to say that in philosophy it matters a great deal where you begin from, and in what order you arrange your discussion. For example, suppose that you and I are both writing something about the relation between society and the individual. You are an individualist: you begin from the existing human individual, and work your way towards an understanding of how a group of such individuals come to function together *as a society*. I on the other hand am a socialist. I take society to be the primary reality, and I then work my way towards an understanding of how the individual, despite being so profoundly embedded in society, can differentiate himself away from society sufficiently to be able to think for and as just *himself*. It is clear, I think, that you and I, moving in opposite directions over the same ground, will end up telling very different stories. The result will *feel* very different in the two cases.

Another example of the kind has been arising during the course of our discussion so far. I have been thinking of the whole history of humanity as a struggle in which all of us, both together and separately, are trying to come to ourselves. At first, the human situation is too overwhelming and bewildering to be clearly thought, head-on. We have to make a long detour through what I call 'heterologous thinking'.[45] We find that we can proceed only by learning to think in an objectifying and mythological way. So I imagine a God who is completely in control. He knows what the world is, and he knows what I am. He knows how I can fit in, and what's good for me. Then, as I think about God and worship him, I start to learn from him. The idea of God gradually *educates* me, so that, after millennia of theological thinking, I can gradually get clearer about what the world is, how it can be known and controlled, what I am, how I should fit in and so on. By this route, God – or at least, the idea of God – gradually enlightens the human race, and then begins a very long process of handing over his powers and perfections to us.[46] The crux of the whole story is the moment when understanding of and power over *the moral order itself* is transferred from God to the human heart. Now the fully emancipated type of human being – 'the last Adam' – begins to emerge at last.

This moment is the hinge of history, in the teaching of Jesus. For the next 17 or 18 centuries the two types of thinking, heterological and autological, coexist and debate with each other. At the Enlightenment the critical kind of thinking triumphs, in natural science, in critical history, in philosophy, and then eventually becomes completely dominant in the modern university. Fully autologous thinking becomes the norm everywhere, at least among the educated, and we begin to look back on the strange history that has produced us.

One of the most conspicuous changes of all is the shift in the sphere of ethics. The old residually theological ethics of objective law comes to be replaced by a new kind of ethics, centred in and upon the individual human being, now seen as being thoroughly embedded in society and history. The main themes are familiar to everyone: liberal democracy, human rights, the ethical state, worldwide humanitarian concern, and a passion for expressive freedom. I am suggesting that in our present cultural situation Jesus can now be recognized as the most important early pioneer of our new radical-humanist type of ethics. Thus although he was only human he remains on our present account the hinge of history.

But now a puzzle arises. Understandably we want to tell a Great Story about the long history out of which we have fairly recently emerged and become ourselves. It is the story of a long transition from heterological to autological thinking. But from which point of view is *the story itself* to be told? If we tell it from the heterological point of view it will be the story of God and God's gradual *kenosis*, or self-emptying, as step-by-step over the centuries he transfers his own powers to us. God's incarnation or 'self-enhistorization' in Jesus will be the hinge, the central event. But if we tell the same story from the autological point of view it will sound very different. It will sound as if humans have dragged themselves up out of pre-conscious darkness by projecting out the idea of a controlling supernatural world. They refined this early theology until they reached full ethical monotheism. This fully developed idea of God gave us humans all our basic ideas, including our ideas of creativity, of a coherent, law-governed world, of knowledge, and of a coherent, rational moral order. Bit by bit, we expropriated God and made his powers and attributes our own. Now he's only an empty shell, a metaphor for an absolute knowledge and perfection that doesn't exist and cannot be attained by us, but still has some value as a guiding ideal. Indeed, I still think it reasonable to be grateful to God for having made us what we are, and our world what it is.

So here are two Grand Narratives, one telling of the gracious *kenosis* or self-emptying of a loving God, and the other telling of the ascent of humankind. Both stories intersect in Jesus, who is on both accounts the hinge of history: but we see now that he is somewhat ambivalent. In a brutally punning sense, he is at the *cross*roads. The theological story makes him the Eternal Word of God incarnate, and the expression of God's self-emptying love for human beings. The radical humanist story makes Jesus a figure more like Prometheus or Lucifer, one who seizes for human beings the greatest gift of all, sovereignty over the moral order itself, and therefore pure expressive and creative freedom. Just as a human moral teacher, he took the boldest step of all in the long process of the making of modern humans.

This explains why we noted early on that in Christian iconography the risen Christ and Lucifer are indistinguishable figures. The former is 'the only-begotten Son of God', and the latter is the greatest and most beautiful of all the angelic sons of God. You could even see them as neighbours in the Great Chain of Being. But the ambiguity is persistently emphasized in Christian iconography. In Revelation 22.16 Jesus is 'the bright Morning Star'; that is, the planet Venus, Lucifer the light-bringer. Picking up the line, a popular hymn calls upon the 'brightest and best of the sons of the morning' – that is, Lucifer himself – to guide us to Jesus.[47]

This casts an interesting sidelight upon Blake's famous and brilliant observation that the greatest English poet – or, at least, the *grandest* English poet – John Milton 'was of the Devil's party without knowing it'. Milton himself stood at a hinge or crux, because he was one of the very last major geniuses who could be and try to remain a fully orthodox Christian. This, despite the fact that he knew what was coming: in his youth, 30-odd years before writing *Paradise Lost*, he had visited the aged Galileo, and the great epic includes discussion of the new science then steadily elbowing the old cosmology aside. But critics have been even more struck by Milton's treatment of the two 'Sons of God', Lucifer/Satan and Christ, the greatest of the burning Seraphs and the Only-Begotten Son of the Father. Where did Milton's sympathies really lie? In 1649 he had defended the execution of the King, taken a post in the new Parliamentary government, and even had written a tract called *Eikonoklastes* (the 'iconoclast', i.e. icon- or image-breaker). It would be surprising if all this personal history did *not* give a certain edginess to Milton's writing of both Lucifer's soliloquies and Jesus' temptations. Are they not *both of them* aspiring to escape from a traditional Divine Order and to achieve a certain exalted form of spiritual freedom? Could they even be like two faces of the same figure, the Morning Star, the brightest of the stars, which hangs low and brilliant in the eastern sky until it is eclipsed by the rising sun?

It's true: a certain ambivalence hangs over the figure of Christ all through the Christian tradition. It is foreshadowed even from the very beginning in the widely divergent reactions he seems to have provoked. In this present essay, I am finding that I can with some confidence make out a *philosophical* case for holding that the early sayings-traditions justify our seeing in Jesus an important precursor of our own modern radical humanism or emotivism in ethics. But when I try to go on and write Jesus so interpreted into a new *religious* Grand Narrative, then I am in trouble, because he turns out to be crucified at the crossroads where two very different and ferociously opposed Grand Narratives meet.

One story is revisionist-Christian. It sees in the whole Story-of-Everything the story of a Love that has created us and then emptied itself, giving itself to us gradually in a long educational process. The final gift is God's gift to us of his very self in Christ, the gift that completely liberates us. This great theological narrative tells us how we can best understand what we are. It needs continual re-enactment in liturgy because it is a profoundly *productive* story.

The other story is a story of how *we*, unconscious of how we were doing it, climbed out of the primeval mud and began our long struggle to become ourselves. We did it by inventing heterological thinking, postulating a supernatural world, and endowing it with all the powers and perfections that we obscurely longed to attain. We aspired upwards. Then, gradually, we ourselves have *ingested*, bit by bit, everything that we had pictured as being out-there. Jesus' teaching set in motion the last stages of the long process. When we have fully assimilated it, we will be able at last to be, consciously, just ourselves, and to love life and each other with open eyes, in simple acceptance of the truth at last.

The first story is the epic about the self-giving of God: the second story is about the roundabout route we had to take in order to become ourselves. Some other stories are also possible. The clash between them is painful, but I do not think we will ever be able finally to resolve the difference. We have no absolute point of view: there *are* no absolutes. So Jesus is stuck with his own ambiguity/ambivalence, as indeed we all are. And we should not complain, because the ambiguity is a powerful stimulant to art and to creative thought.

An intriguing question to end this chapter: was Jesus himself aware of his own ambivalence? There is a suggestion to that effect in the idea of the prophet who understands – perhaps from the outset – that his destiny is to be one who is rejected by the very people to whom he is sent; and there is another example in the dispute about the power by which Jesus performs exorcisms. Is it 'the finger of God', or is it 'Beelzebul' (Q/Luke 11.19f.)? But there is also a third example. Ancient thought was much impressed by the way a great fire on earth can be kindled by lightning-strike. Very interestingly, there are goodish sayings by Jesus that apply this metaphor *both* to Satan *and* to himself (see the 'fire on earth' saying in *Thomas* 10 and Q/Luke 12.49, and the saying about Satan's fall in Luke 10.18). Wow! Then in the following sayings (Luke 12.51–53, well attested in Q and *Thomas*) there is a certain tragic awareness of his own ambivalence on Jesus' part. His message of peace causes bitter conflict; his moral passion for a world without *ressentiment* provokes a storm of *ressentiment* against himself.

In general, Jesus' message was not about himself at all. But in these four fairly well attested sayings there does seem to be more than a hint that Jesus was aware of a certain tragic irony in his own position – just as Old Testament figures such as Jeremiah and Jonah had been.

16

The Nihilist

I cannot at present think of any other ordinary human being known to us whose ethical vision was as overwhelmingly strong as that of Jesus. It was so strong that it violently overrode even the highest of moral obligations as they are generally recognized, such as the duty to care for and be loyal to one's own parents and other kinsfolk. He tells his disciples to abandon their parents, and repudiates his own kin when they come looking for him and saying that he is off his head.[48] Jesus' ethical vision was so strong that he was perfectly ready, if necessary, to 'disrespect' revealed Divine Law, such as the laws governing Sabbath observance and ritual purity. And along with his consciously lax attitude to religious law went uncompromising disrespect for religious professionals, and for religious institutions such as the Temple.

Further, as I have emphasized, in some of his best-known and best-attested parables, such as those of the Labourers in the Vineyard, the Talents, and the Unjust Steward, as well as in many other texts to the same effect, Jesus sharply criticizes and even ridicules ordinary people's ideas about justice and equity. (He does this, it seems, because ordinary people's ideas about justice *themselves* produce ill-feeling, as witness the 'victim impact statements' made in our courts of law.)

So sharply does Jesus emphasize the discontinuity between ordinary, established moral and religious reality and his own new ethical vision that it is not surprising that he should seem to be subverting existing reality completely. He is a *transgressor*, someone who 'walks across' and violates deeply drawn social lines and boundaries. Tradition indicates that for a short period at the beginning of his public activity Jesus may have been a follower of John the Baptist, but once he is established in his own short career Jesus is always an *anti-traditionalist* and a *nonconformist*, and never a docile, conforming 'sheep'. He is always a leader and never a follower; always a person consumed by his vision of an entirely new reality, and never someone who can be deflected from his course by arguments to the effect that existing reality is objectively fixed and cannot be changed by mere acts of human will. On the contrary, says Jesus, when we have the courage to drop everything and decide for his new world, then the new world will have come into being.

We now see something of the fully philosophical implications of Jesus' commanding ethical vision. He is not a rationalist and realist, who wants us to regard existing reality as fixed and rational, and to stay within its bounds. He wants us to step outside existing reality and choose a new world. He is, in effect, a *nihilist* – a person who refuses all existing reality – and an extreme *voluntarist*, someone who insists that if we choose a new world with sufficient decisiveness, then we'll find ourselves in that new world. In the crudest modern English, 'life's what you make it'.

How is this possible? Jesus' teaching gives a hint, because he is also in philosophy an *expressivist*. He doesn't see the human mind as mirroring or reflecting nature-out-there, and he doesn't see the good life as a life that conforms to a 'natural moral law', out-there and independent of us. On the contrary, he sees everything as flowing *out from us*, as in the sharp exchange about what makes a person unclean.[49] It is not what goes *into* him, says Jesus, it's what comes *out* of a man's heart that makes a man clean or unclean. We don't mirror our world: our world mirrors *us*.

Jesus' expressivism means that he sees the good life as being more like the life of an artist than the life of a soldier. A soldier is a conformist who fits happily into a readymade reality. The soldier is like a Roman Catholic: he likes discipline, he likes to have his own place in a strong community, and he loves to have everything that troubles him already decided for him. But the artist is a lover of freedom, who needs plenty of space and malleable material, so that he can build a new world, the world he dreams of. The artist is an 'aestheticist', someone for whom the world around us is a work of folk art that has been slowly built up by us. He'd like at least to question, and probably to change, the way we ordinarily see it.

We usually think of expressivism as a very modern and radical doctrine, scarcely even intelligible before the Romantic Movement. How was Jesus, living as and when he did, able to come up with such an idea? The answer given by the best tradition of Jesus' own teaching is that he was a very visual person, strongly committed to and influenced by the ancient prescientific idea of how our vision works.

This point is important, because we are often misled by the cliché to the effect that whereas the Greeks were a people of the eye, the Jews were a people of the ear. The Greeks love the 'shining' (or, in Greek, 'phenomenal') visual beauty of sculpture and architecture, whereas the Jews love the word and music. Not quite right, because the best tradition of Jesus' teaching reveals a predominantly visual 'metaphoric', with music nowhere. He clearly saw the I in terms of the eye, as many of us do, and he was reinforced in this habit by the fact that for him (as for almost everyone up to and including John Donne[50]) the eye was like a torch or a lamp, which emits a strong 'eyebeam', just like the beam of a powerful torch.[51] In ordinary language to this day we still speak of the gaze as a powerful scanning beam. It 'sweeps the horizon', it 'falls' and 'rests upon' this or that, or it may only 'alight' or 'light' briefly upon something. Thus for the prescientific world our vision is active, *illuminating*: it lights up the world and makes it intelligible. And of course Jesus' own expressivism leads him to say that we too should be radiant, glowing like lamps shining prominently in a public place. We should put on a good show. We should sparkle, a point I tried to make in the book *Solar Ethics* of 1995 by using a highly *visual* meta-phoric modelled upon that of Jesus.

There's yet one more piece to the jigsaw, and then Jesus' philosophy will begin to cohere. From Plato to Kant, and in many respects until much more recently, nearly all of Western thought was shaped by the appearance/reality distinction. This distinction contrasts the outward, visible, superficial, transient appearance of things with their inner, deeper, unseen, more valuable and lasting Reality. Although we tend to associate the distinction chiefly with Plato and Greek metaphysics, it is also prominent in the Bible. In 1 Samuel, for example, the outward appearance that a person sees is contrasted with the heart, which God sees, and Paul draws a similar contrast between the outward person who is perishing, and the inner person – the inner reality of the self – which never grows old but is renewed day by day.[52] But Jesus seems almost entirely to lack the appearance/reality distinction.

There are two *prima facie* counter-examples to be dealt with. One is the contrast Jesus draws between what is hidden and what is revealed. This however is not in the least Platonic. The hidden is not the deeper, more precious and lasting reality of a thing here at all: rather it is our dark secrets, our sins and so on, which will certainly be searched out and brought to light by the all-seeing eye of God. In the Kingdom-world everything is bathed in light and nothing can remain hidden. Everything will be wide open to view.

The second counter-example that might be cited is the contrast between perishable earthly treasures and the imperishable treasure that the wise are busy laying up for themselves in heaven. This is certainly profoundly Platonic, but for that very reason clearly cannot be part of Jesus' own thinking. A ludicrously Platonic exegesis of Jesus was still very common in Victorian times, when preachers assured their hearers that a parable was 'an earthly story with a heavenly meaning', and would claim that in all his teaching Jesus was transforming the mere ritual outwardness of Jewish observances and laws into the spiritual inwardness of Christianity. No doubt with memories of all those errors, the Jesus Seminar scholars regarded all the treasure-on-earth-versus-treasure-in-heaven sayings as contemporary popular wisdom that has been rather unthinkingly ascribed to Jesus – which is surely correct.[53]

I conclude this section of the discussion by insisting that in philosophy Jesus was profoundly anti-Platonic – at least, by implication. He does not urge us to turn away from the superficial appearance of things and seek instead a deeper, invisible and eternal Reality behind it. No, he urges us to choose a new moral world in which everything is clear and brightly lit, and there *is* no invisible, 'deep' reality. In morality Jesus wants a world that is completely open, explicit, *clarus* (bright and clear), because he correctly sees that ill-feeling is very often *double*-feeling. Consider words like malice, deceit, deception, duplicity, falsity, hypocrisy, insincerity, flattery and so on. They all imply a certain doubleness: we maintain a gap between our displayed feelings and real but veiled feelings and intentions that are hidden behind them. The attraction of angels both in Dante and in Milton is that they are completely transparent. You can see right through them, so that they cannot lie to you or deceive you. Children are similarly commended by Jesus for their *artlessness*, or candour.

Now we see why Jesus' commanding vision is profoundly anti-Platonic, and can even appear nihilistic. His longing for pure moral clarity is so great that he must reject our present world, with its various levels of openness and hiddenness, its ubiquitous veiled ill-feeling, its reservations and its meanness of spirit. Instead, he yearns for pure mutuality, openness, candour in a social world in which nothing is or can be murky, or hidden, or on the back-burner, or deferred.

Such an intense moral passion is exceedingly rare among human beings. Elsewhere I have already used the relevant analogy, but I cannot resist using it again. Ethics is to metaphysics as sculpture is to painting, and as biology is to physics. In the West, we've had dozens of great physicists, but only a handful of great biological theorists (one could be forgiven for saying, only one) – yet biology is greater than physics. We have had hundreds of great painters, but only a handful of truly great sculptors (perhaps only four: three Italians and a Frenchman) – yet sculpture is greater than painting. And in philosophy we have had two dozen or more great metaphysicians, but scarcely a single great and passionate ethical theorist (there's one candidate, a German) – yet ethics is the greatest subject of all.

Jesus' vision might be very coarsely described as a form of utopian radical humanism. Within a generation of his death it had become very badly occluded by the cult of his person, and the consequent blurring of the tradition of his teaching. But it has survived well enough to have hugely influenced humankind, and its influence has grown greatly since the happy decline of church Christianity.[54] We can now begin to see it more clearly.

17

Choosing Life

The method used in this book is straightforward. To recapitulate, we have received by various routes a large body of ancient documents of very varied quality that purport to give us information about the life and the teaching of Jesus. This material has been closely studied by thousands of scholars for a couple of centuries or so by now. I have accepted the current consensus, to the effect that nearly everything that is of historical value is to be found in the Gospels of Matthew, Mark, Luke and *Thomas*, and I have accepted the standard view of the literary relationships between these four texts.

I have also presumed that some of the traditions about Jesus' teachings are better and more reliable than the traditions about his life. The main reason for this is that Jesus' method of publication seems to have been to compose a substantial body of parables and epigrammatic sayings. These he taught to his disciples, for them to transmit orally. Like jokes, such anecdotes need to be repeated accurately, or the audience will rightly complain that they don't understand the point of them. Sayings such as 'Love your enemies' or 'The first will be last, and the last first' are not easily misremembered. They stick in the mind.

The traditions about Jesus' *life*, however, do not inspire the same confidence. At first, it seems, Jesus was remembered and venerated only as a teacher, and the first 'Gospels' were produced simply as written collections of sayings that had been received by oral tradition. The gospel form as we know it was invented by Mark around the year 70. It follows in detail the standard pattern for the life of an Eastern holy man, whether Indian or Mediterranean,[55] and itself often admits in the text that its own narratives are 'fulfilments of scripture' – that is, have been worked up from Old Testament sources. Furthermore, Mark himself is highly tendentious. His work reflects the fast-growing supernatural theology of the early Christian community and the power struggles between different factions and leaders within it. Most revealing of all is Mark's picture of the so-called 'Messianic Secret'. Mark's Jesus knows he is the Christ, but charges his disciples not to tell anyone – thus clearly trying to forestall the objections of readers who will surely complain that all this elaborate supernatural theology about Jesus is suspiciously new. Why have we not heard about it before, and why was it not in the long-established sayings-traditions that we have been familiar with for years?

Jesus' life then is late theological fiction, but there is a good chance that we may find something interesting in the sayings-traditions. During the past 30 years much of the best scholarship has been American. In Europe, too much of biblical scholarship has been in effect politically controlled by the churches and by local politicians, especially in the German Länder, whereas in America there is commonly a much happier convention, which has denominational theology taught in the seminaries to ordinands, while fully independent critical scholarship can flourish in the university departments of religion, for the most part without any threat of interference.

In the USA, the leading Jesus-scholars during the past 30 years have been E. P. Sanders and John Dominic Crossan. I have used their work, but most of all I have liked the systematic clarity and transparency of the work, and the presented conclusions, of Robert W. Funk's large 'Jesus Seminar' group of scholars, who worked under the aegis of Funk's Westar Institute at Santa Rosa, California, chiefly between 1986 and 1993, and were sometimes co-chaired by Crossan.

So I have read their publications, and have tried to listen with a philosopher's ear to all the material that in the final report (1993) of the Seminar was rated as being of the greatest historical value.

I listened out for a strong, coherent and individual voice with a high-quality message, and believe that I have found it. Thirty years ago, I recall arguing that although we have almost no critical-historical knowledge of the Buddha because we have no documents that are anything like early enough, there must surely have been an outstanding individual mind somewhere at the beginning of the Buddhist tradition, and it is reasonable to name this mind 'the Buddha'. Similarly, if I find an outstanding and coherent individual ethical vision at the centre of all the oldest surviving Jesus-traditions, it is reasonable to attach the name of Jesus to this vision.

Accordingly, I have concluded that Jesus was an almost secular moral teacher, whose teaching was entirely concerned with attempting by all means to persuade his hearers to drop everything and commit themselves wholeheartedly to a quite new moral world, a human-life-world with no shadows, no lurking ill-feeling or *ressentiment*, a world in which everything is open to view and is exactly what it presents itself as being, and a world ruled by love, in which everyone lives from and by the heart. This radical-humanist utopia Jesus called 'the Reign of God'. He took the idea from Jewish tradition, but did not add any independent teaching about what he supposed 'God' to be. Presumably it seemed unnecessary to do so, in that context.

Jesus' ethical teaching is extraordinary, and extraordinarily demanding. In the English tradition there have been just a few people who seem to echo Jesus' style of thinking and speaking, namely the William Blake of *The Everlasting Gospel* and lyrics such as 'The Divine Image' in *Songs of Innocence*, and the later Wittgenstein in his philosophy of ordinary language. There are one or two other possible names: when young, I was once lucky enough to have an hour talking *à deux* with Stanley Spencer in front of his paintings as they hung in Cookham Church at his last major retrospective. Spencer was a bit like Jesus, too, albeit in an eccentrically English way.

As for the Christian Church and its religion, that is something rather different, but by parallel reasoning one might guess that its chief inventor was probably Paul. He evidently had the energy, the theological imagination and the psychological power to collect and systematize a whole lot of floating scraps, which we see coming together into something like a coherent theology in his first letter to the Thessalonians, of about the year 51.

Paul, however, has not been our concern here. His religion, for good or ill, seems now to be finally passing away. But what of Jesus' ethical vision, now re-emerging after having been somewhat occluded for the past 19 centuries? Is it big enough to stand in its own right as a major event in the history of ethics; and to what school in moral philosophy should we assign Jesus? What was his world-view?

I think Jesus' message is genuinely remarkable. So grand and memorable is it that its historical outworking has continued to the present day. Indeed, no other moralist anywhere has had so wide and enduring an influence upon people's social hopes. The world he wanted us to choose remains the kind of world that liberal democrats, socialists, anarchists, syndicalists, Tolstoyans, communists and modern humanitarians have laboured to build. He profoundly influenced the original dream of 'America', a dream that as I write has been revived yet again by the election of the country's first black president, the dream of a society highly variegated but fully fraternal and completely free, a society in which the daily lives of the most ordinary people would be invested with epic simplicity and dignity.

As for Jesus' *philosophy*, the first and most important point to be grasped is what is implied by putting ethics first in his uniquely thoroughgoing way. He is already moving well away from the old custom of deriving ethics from cosmology – and in particular, of seeing the moral life in terms of conformity to religious Law, which in turn is grounded in a religion-based cosmology. No: Jesus, like us, lives at the end of that kind of world, which is why we called him a nihilist who demands of us a peculiarly absolute kind of ethical choice (the Bible calls it 'choosing life'[56]). In terms of recent Anglo-Saxon moral philosophy Jesus is an emotivist and a voluntarist, and in terms of English poetry he asks us to 'live from the heart'. Even today, many people will insist that moral idealism cannot make any headway in the face of unchangeable facts about 'human nature' or 'the real world'. But Jesus puts the moral demand for a better world first, and does not think of bowing to 'the facts'.

How could an ordinary human being of that remote place and time have had such stupendously grand thoughts? It would appear that Jesus simply radicalized a familiar theme he found in the Hebrew prophets, namely God's promise to relocate himself within the human heart. 'I will put my spirit within you', 'I will write my law upon your hearts', 'I will take away your heart of stone and give you a heart of flesh', 'I myself will be with you and in you'. When everything is internalized within the self, God dies, the world comes to an end, and I am confronted with the need to make an absolute choice, which is a repetition of God's original choice to create the world out of nothing. Inevitably, as modern Western thought has approached nihilism, 'existentialist' writers have appeared who have learnt what it is like to be absolutely alone and confronted with the need to make an absolute choice, *God's* choice, the choice of life itself; and when we get into this territory we are apt to start finding the historical Jesus interesting again.

My procedure invites three comments that are sure to be made, and which may or may not turn out to embody serious objections to my arguments and conclusions. There is the *Albert Schweitzer objection*, there is the *question about Q* and its theology, and there is a question about *how far Paul misread Jesus*.

The *Albert Schweitzer objection* runs as follows: In his *Von Reimarus zu Wrede* of 1906, translated into *The Quest of the Historical Jesus* (1913), Schweitzer argued that the 150-year-long attempt to rediscover the Jesus of history by using the methods of critical history had failed. The hope had been that the original Jesus when found would transform and renew Christianity, but the hope was disappointed. The original Jesus had indeed been found – but he was quite irrelevant to us. His teaching had been completely dominated by the belief that very soon, amid world-wide tribulations, history would come to a violent end with the coming down to earth upon the clouds of heaven of the Son of Man . . . and so on. We could not possibly revert to such a remote and strange world-view.

Schweitzer called his theory 'thoroughgoing' or 'consistent eschatology'. It came to prevail, and many of the orthodox came to accept the view of Rudolf Bultmann that the life and teaching of the historical Jesus had belonged entirely to the history of late ancient Judaism. Christian faith and the Christian preaching had begun only *after* Easter morning, and not before. Jesus himself and his teaching were not very interesting: he had been merely the failed prophet of a *supernatural* Kingdom of God.

Having been so influential for a whole century, Schweitzer's theory has itself become a kind of orthodoxy to which many of the orthodox themselves cling out of long habit. Its uncomfortableness is a discomfort that they have got used to, and so they stick to it obstinately.

But was Schweitzer correct? Read carefully through Q with the help of John S. Kloppenborg's *Q Parallels*, or in the English translation if you wish. The verdict is unavoidable: on the one hand, it is true, as I have said, that the parables and the reversal-sayings, that on any view were central to Jesus' teaching, appear to be secular-humanist in their assumptions and their 'machinery'; but on the other hand, it must be admitted that Q also contains a good deal of *early* eschatology. Q's doctrine of Christ is very undeveloped, but Q's Jesus does seem to use apocalyptic imagery about a coming Day of Judgement. He ends by promising his own faithful disciples that they will sit upon thrones, judging the twelve tribes of Israel.[57]

I'm not worried. The technical details can be left to the New Testament specialists, many of whom will retort that the eschatological material in Q belongs to its latest stratum, and *not* to the earliest, Galilean, layer, but I have already coped with Schweitzer's main thesis by translating his 'thorough-going eschatology' into the simpler and far clearer language of philosophy by saying that (in an exceptionally thorough-going way) Jesus 'put ethics first'. That is all that need be said, and I am surprised that Schweitzer, an energetic and able young man who had written a doctoral dissertation on *Kant's Philosophy of Religion*, could not see something so obvious. Kant balanced nature and morality, the worldly put nature first, and Jesus put morality first – in a very radical way. Zoroastrian and Jewish eschatology and apocalyptic is the natural idiom of ordinary non-philosophical people who see everything in terms of a cosmic battle between good and evil, and who passionately wish to see the suffering righteous vindicated. They will not let any supposedly fixed natural facts stand in the way of the realization of their ethical dream. *In that sense*, ordinary folk also put ethics first. Jesus is perfectly ready to use the same language himself, but his version of the philosophical doctrine that ethics comes first of all states that individuals must be challenged deliberately to choose the new moral world for themselves, and then by their own absolute choice of it they will bring the new world into being. Perhaps people have been thrown by Jesus' un-nerving and even frightening way of radicalizing everything that he touches. Intellectually, he can be ferocious.

In any case, my answer to the *Albert Schweitzer objection* is that Jesus put ethics first – and even radicalizes that slogan itself. Such a 'double radicalization' is a common trick in Buddhist religious thought, but Christians have been very dim, and it has to be said that much of twentieth-century theology rested upon a mistake. Jesus was not 'irrelevant' to us. His relation to his own cultural setting was analogous to Nietzsche's relation to the nineteenth-century European bourgeoisie. For both, 'we can't go on like this': existing reality is unendurable, and we must choose something different, soon.

Something similar should perhaps be said in reply to the *question about Q*. The consensus nowadays is that Q, so far as we can reconstruct it, well reflects the state of the Jesus-tradition round about the years 50–70. It doesn't know about the destruction of the Temple, and its doctrine of Christ is very undeveloped compared with that of Paul. Perhaps Q is closer to the Galilean community, whereas Paul's ideas were being worked out *ambulando* as he wandered around the Graeco-Roman world, disputing in the synagogues of the diaspora, and starting his own little groups.

The *question about Q* is this: I have emphasized that in the core tradition of his parables and sayings Jesus is completely without self-concern. His message is *never* about himself. Like John, he's just a voice, calling us to make an ethical decision for the 'Reign of God'. So why did the huge cult of Jesus' *person* ever develop, and why is it that in Q there are already some passages that seem to show it emerging? There is even one startling passage (Q 10.21–22; Matthew 11.25–27; Luke 10.21, 22) in which Jesus actually talks in the idiom of St John's Gospel. But in addition there are passages that illustrate the early Christian community's developing theology of his person and his role in the economy of salvation.

It was probably unavoidable. Jesus was very reticent about himself, probably, but our whole cultural tradition has always been prone to what I earlier described as the Derrida-mistake – the tendency mistakenly to believe that Jesus' own words, when read aloud, somehow mediate to us his living presence. To this day, believers stand and face 'the Gospel' when it is read at the Eucharist. In early Christian art, in Byzantium, and indeed upon any Christian altar, the Gospel-book stands for Jesus himself. The sad result was that the words of Jesus lost their human interest and complexity and declined into being something more like the oracles of a god. Jesus' teaching became 'the law of Christ', and so contributed to a reinstatement of the religion of Divine Law that he had sought to supersede. By deifying Jesus, the Church destroyed almost everything he stood for.

Sadly, the cult of Jesus' person has diminished him, and in the long run seems to have made him a curiously embarrassing figure, weak, reproachful and androgynous. As for the Jesus of St John's Gospel who delivers lengthy and awkward speeches about himself, saying that 'I am' this or that, he reminds us of the feminist Christmas card on which one sister observes to another: 'After all, the birth of a man who thinks he's God is not exactly an unusual event.'

What of the third question, that about *how far Paul misread Jesus*? There is a very long tradition that regards Paul as a villain. 'Jesus preached the Kingdom, but what we got was the Church', people say. But it is worth replying that Paul did rather successfully preserve in his system at least *some* of Jesus' leading ideas.

First, by successfully arguing that the Torah need not be imposed upon Gentile converts, Paul retained Jesus' own merely instrumental view of the Law. The rabbis had indeed themselves already taught that in the Kingdom of God the Torah and the sacrificial system would give way to a new era of grace in which the only sacrifice still offered would be the sacrifice of praise and thanksgiving (that is, the 'Eucharist'). So Paul evidently saw at least a partial realization of the Kingdom in the Church.

Second, by strongly insisting upon God's pure gift to us of a grace and forgiveness that are quite unmerited, Paul keeps a vital bit of Jesus' ethics in his own systematic theology. In accordance with his usual pattern of argument, Paul argues that if God has shown quite unmerited graciousness to *us*, then we too in our turn ought now to be up to showing something of the same pure generosity to others. So far as it goes this is quite good, but of course it falls well short of Jesus' own purely ethical – and very original – insight that ordinary ideas of law and justice can never build and maintain full social peace. In order to break the chain of tit-for-tat retaliation, every human being has got to understand that it is necessary to be *oneself* capable on occasion of taking the initiative with an act of pure, spontaneous and supererogatory generosity and forgiveness. Paul compromises the ethics of Jesus by putting his own theology in front of it. He puts God's initiative first, and makes our moral action a response to it. But for Jesus our moral initiative will not convince others, and will have no moral power, unless it really is spontaneous and from the heart. Everyone sees that that is true in the erotic realm: it is also true in matters of justice and reconciliation.

In parenthesis, many thinkers have talked of going 'beyond good and evil', of 'the teleological suspension of the ethical', and so on. This is dangerous territory, and I insist upon sticking close to Jesus' own account, which I think is right. There have been many examples of the moral and psychological problems involved in the recent history of ethnic conflicts in Northern Ireland, in the former Yugoslavia, and elsewhere.

In conclusion, then, we may acknowledge that Jesus does indeed have a background and setting in late ancient Judaism, and that he did contribute at least something to the teaching of the early Church. So he is a fully historical figure with his own *Sitz-im-Leben* (setting in life); but it does not follow that he must be considered 'dated'. On the contrary, from a strictly philosophical point of view his ethical teaching is very remarkable, and in many ways is as interesting and challenging to us today as ever it was in the past.

How? I think the answer has to do with the question of the absolute and the merely relative in ethical theory generally, and in the framing of one's own life. In almost any period, individuals are apt to feel overshadowed by fear and dread of something absolute that looms before them and seems to annihilate everything else. Ordinary life is a web of relative priorities, obligations and valuations. It requires us to do a kind of balancing act, keeping many different plates spinning at once. But the absolute may give us the horrors because it seems completely to destroy our ordinary housewifely ability to cope with and balance our manifold everyday duties. It reduces everything to rubble.

This annihilating absolute, for many people nowadays, takes the form of a general fear of the ultimate 'meaninglessness' and emptiness of all human life just as such. Or it may take the form of suddenly learning that one has a terminal illness and will very soon be dead. Alternatively, one may feel that the scale of human wickedness and suffering is becoming so vast that it can be endured no longer. A violent apocalyptic End of all things is desperately needed, and indeed must soon come. People can get themselves into a state of being *hungry* for war and general destruction. Or again, one may have a rational science-based conviction that the human race will not survive for more than another century or two. Why are we still begetting and bearing children? The impending, annihilating absolute may take many forms. Maybe it is only a coloured-up contemporary version of something that philosophy has always known and described as the radical contingency of all finite existence. But, in whatever form, most of us today are aware of it, as perhaps most people always have been. And when we confront it, the ethical teaching of Jesus is interesting and relevant.

The brilliantly lit focal point is this: In the old mythology, God, confronted by the Primal Chaos, by a free and purely generous act of will *chose* to conquer chaos and create the world. The Israelite prophets saw the religious problem – namely, the infinite qualitative difference between the Holy God and the wayward human individual – as being solved when God relocates himself within the human heart. Jesus takes that thought and radicalizes it, in order to force upon the individual a repetition of the original creative choice. When I feel that everything is crumbling and I am confronted with pure chaos, I have to make a free, generous and founding choice of life itself. This original choice, a choice to launch oneself bravely out upon the sea of contingent existence, comes from what we speak of as 'the heart'. By it we live.

18

The Slow-Working Dream

At the beginning of this book we made a contrast between two types of ethical theory. The broadly 'theological' type of ethic models morality upon law, and in particular, *religious* law. The whole world is like a superstate, whose king of kings is God. God's will for his human subjects is expressed in a large and systematic body of law. Some of it, traditionally called the 'natural moral law', is built into and enforced by the way the world works – God's 'moral providence' – and there is also a supplementary body of 'revealed' religious law, often seen as having been dictated by God himself or by an angel acting on God's behalf. The religious founder who has 'heard' and written down the scriptural revelation is seen as a great lawgiver and prophet, such as Moses.

In antiquity the local law-code was often carved upon big flat 'tables' of stone and erected in a public place, rather as to this day in Britain the locally applicable by-laws are sometimes to be seen posted up in public places such as parks and railway stations. Ancient stones with law-codes inscribed upon them can still be seen re-erected on site at Gortys in Crete, and there are of course several examples in the British Museum.

From this background people have inherited the idea that a good, sound ethic will take the form of a system of rules that is known to everyone because it is either evident to conscience or prominently published, and is binding upon everyone. Everyone is equal before the law, in the sense that everyone must obey it. It binds all the king's subjects into a complex network of reciprocal rights and duties, that is, a *society*; and

above all, it is already in force. This is a conservative concep-
tion of morality: it functions to ratify the social status quo.

Every form of moral realism or objectivism ultimately
rests upon this background, and can therefore be described
as being 'residually theological'. The moral standard is out
there, it is one, objective, and universal, in one way or another
it is known to all those who are bound by it, it creates and
maintains an ordered society, and it is a given, an established
social fact. I have contrasted this grand, traditional, objective legalism with our modern humanist ethics which tries
instead to make human beings themselves the only makers of
their own 'lifestyles'. The universe as such is not moral, the
main reason for this opinion being that the colossal success
of modern natural science depended from the outset upon its
setting aside of all ideas of purposiveness and built-in value.
Nature is just machinery. Human beings have been thrown
back upon themselves, and have learnt to talk always of
human values, *human* rights, *human* needs, and of *humanitarian* concerns. Ethics, being now only human, no longer
comes ready-made, cosmic and immutable. On the contrary,
it is humanly improvised and continually changing. It is *from
the heart.*

To me, this human and conventional character of modern ethics is exhilarating. It breathes the air of pure moral
freedom that since the Second World War has enabled us to
bring about huge moral changes. Better health and longer
lives for the common people, at least in the developed countries. More care about the environment. Great advances in
the social and economic emancipation of women, gay people
and many other groups. Even relatively minor things, such as
the Paralympic Games for the disabled, are a source of great
satisfaction. That we humans have in many ways done so
well shows that the new only-human and emotivist approach
to ethics is at least as good as the old objectivist ethics ever
was. And I have claimed that Jesus of Nazareth was a remote
and very remarkable pioneer of our modern humanism. As a
god, he is all washed up now, but as a *man* he has been and

still is so influential as almost to justify the division of all history into the periods before him and after him.

But now we face a serious difficulty. The old objective morality of law had the great advantage of being able to see itself as being *universal*, systematic, applicable to every one of the king's subjects, already in place, and already in force. Everyone must be loyal to it because it maintains the social order, of which it takes a conservative view. But the new kind of morality Jesus tried to introduce takes nothing for granted. It breaks with the whole existing order of human relationships as being radically unsatisfactory. It requires us to drop *everything* and decide for an entirely new world, to be populated by a new kind of human being. (Compare the 'New Man' that socialism at its height tried to create.[58]) In short, Jesus' world-renouncing ethic sounds like the ethic of a band of itinerant, mendicant holy men, such as Buddhist monks or Franciscan friars.

Now, I don't doubt that in some cases the Buddhist way to salvation really works. The *sangha* is a version of the Kingdom of God, an ideal society in which people can learn to live completely without *ressentiment* or ill-feeling. It is a touching idea. So is the ideal of the mendicant Franciscan friar who lives by love. *But who provides their daily food?* Who indeed bears and raises the children from among whom they will recruit their future members? Ultimately it is always lowly Piers Plowman who produces the food, the clothing and so on that the wandering holy man consumes. And it is Piers Plowman and his wife, the common people, who bear and raise the children. Jesus and his band were no exception: they were part of culture, they lived off the agricultural surplus as do all artists, scholars and religious professionals. Much as the holy men condemned the general unsatisfactoriness of the old social order, they required it to continue in existence in order to sustain their dream. As Bernard Shaw once remarked, nothing is more helpful to those who dream of living a bohemian life than a fat quarterly cheque from bourgeois parents.

There is thus a double sense in which what used to be erroneously described as 'the Sermon on the Mount' is 'an impossible ethic'. The traditional, Lutheran sense is that it is too exalted and demanding an ethic for us human beings actually to live by. It functions, as Lutherans have traditionally taught, to convict us of sin and force us to seek salvation by faith alone. As for actually *living* the ethics of Jesus in full, that must be deferred until either the Kingdom comes on earth, or we get to heaven. Not now; certainly not just now.

But there is also another and more serious sense in which the Kingdom-dream seems to be impossible. It seems to be economically impossible. We cannot all live like holy vagabonds (the Russian *yurodivy*), and we cannot *all* of us sell up everything we have. Who would there be to sell *to*? There has to be settled life, there has to be land tenure, there has to be social infrastructure, there has to be economic exchange, and of course there has to be Piers Plowman, toiling away in the fields every day and carrying the rest of the world on his back. And in view of all this, is it not obvious that there will have to be some sort of compromise between the two moralities? The old theological morality of religious law binds everyone into maintaining the existing social order, while the dream morality is kept as 'pie in the sky' and as a distant hope of future blessedness. The compromise might be justifiable – so long as the Dream is not idle, but genuinely influential and productive.

Perhaps one might see the whole history of the Judaeo-Christian culture area since Jesus as a field in which the two moralities have been debating the terms of their necessary compromise with each other. Economic necessity *versus* utopian humanism; respect for the existing social order and your own 'station' in it *versus* the dream of a hippy paradise in which love is all you need; Piers Plowman the humble labourer *versus* the bishop in his palace and the contemplative nun in her cell who are ultimately supported by his toil.

The dilemma is still acute, even today. In a recent book, *The Meaning of the West* (2008), I praised the modern lib-

eral democratic welfare state as the very first society in all of
human history that actually *delivers the Dream,* by provid-
ing a full span of life in modest good health and comfort
to the great mass of unskilled and low-skilled workers, with
the addition of free access to education and a wide range of
cultural production. In short, the modern ethical state is far
kinder to its own weaker members than ever the state was in
the so-called ages of faith. Since 'the Death of God' (around
1680–1720) the liberal democratic state has gradually come
to perform the traditional Corporal Works of Mercy on a
vast scale, and today actually implements much of Jesus'
programme. In the post-Christian epoch, as the Church has
slowly died, the state has become startlingly Christian. The
state's ethics is today much more Christian than is the official
ethics of the churches.

Now the dilemma: the secure and highly esteemed public-
service side of the culture that delivers the emergency services, the health service, education at all levels, the social
services, welfare benefits and all the rest to the people has
become a sort of new 'church', which is actually supported
by heavy taxes levied upon the private sector – the relatively
insecure and disesteemed bankers, businessmen, industri-
alists, managers, salespeople, and ordinary industrial and
agricultural workers who actually generate the wealth that
supports relatively 'superior' types like you and me. It all
bears an eerie resemblance to the relationship between the
religious and the secular realms in the Middle Ages, which is
perhaps why Thatcherite Conservatives and New Labour in
Britain have attempted to befriend the private sector and to
persuade the rest of us that businessmen and bankers are not
just greedy crooks. They lubricate the whole economy and
create the wealth that pays our salaries and our very secure
pensions; and in many ways they are less secure than we
medics, academics, clerics and artists.

This leads me to end by proposing a new, reformulated
distinction, between lawlike morality-systems that seek to
validate and support the existing social order, and our very

long-lived, slow-acting, indelible Dream of a world in which human relationships are far, far better than they usually are now. This dream of a radically better world has been enormously influential amongst us, especially during the past few centuries, and it has generated a huge number of spin-offs. We owe it, most of all, to Jesus of Nazareth.

In conclusion, we now understand that ethics has two different faces or dimensions, which roughly correspond to the doctrines of creation and redemption in traditional theology.

On the 'creation' side ethics is very properly concerned with supporting existing reality. One has a duty to be loyal to the system as it is, keeping the wheels turning, obeying the rules, playing one's part and raising the next generation. Of course morality has to have this 'conservative' face: nobody wants to live in a failed state, as is the dreadful plight of many peoples in Africa today.

But on the 'redemption' side, ethics is also concerned with spelling out and keeping alive the Dream of a better world. If the Dream is sufficiently vivid and attractive, it will shape our values and the orientation of our lives, so that in the very long term it will tend to become self-fulfilling. People usually think of the preaching of Jesus as being very urgent and short-termist, but in fact the opposite has turned out to be the case. His message has begun to produce its best effects only in modern times. He lit a very slow-burning fuse – and he prompts an afterthought: perhaps the nineteenth-century idea that the historical Jesus, when rediscovered, may become the basis for a reform and renewal of Christianity does have a future after all.

Notes

1 Geza Vermes, *Jesus the Jew*, London: Collins, 1973, etc.

2 E. P. Sanders, *The Historical Figure of Jesus*, Harmondsworth: Penguin, 1993.

3 John Dominic Crossan, *The Historical Jesus: The Life of a Mediterranean Jewish Peasant*, San Francisco: Harper, 1991; *Jesus: A Revolutionary Biography*, San Francisco: Harper, 1994.

4 Especially the following three titles: R. W. Funk, Roy W. Hoover and the Jesus Seminar, *The Five Gospels: The Search for the Authentic Words of Jesus*, A Polebridge Press Book, New York: Scribner, 1996; R. W. Funk and the Jesus Seminar, *The Gospel of Jesus, according to the Jesus Seminar*, Santa Rosa, CA: Polebridge Press, 1999; John S. Kloppenborg and Others, *Q/Thomas Reader: The Sayings Gospel Q, and the Gospel of Thomas*, Santa Rosa, CA: Polebridge Press, 1990.

5 John S. Kloppenborg is the leading contemporary interpreter of Q. For a general survey of the present state of the Historical-Jesus question, see David Boulton, *Who On Earth Was Jesus? The Modern Quest for the Jesus of History*, Winchester and Washington: O Books, 2008.

6 The moral argument for the existence of God in J. H. Newman's *Grammar of Assent* is a notorious example of a common fallacy. Newman gives an account of moral experience that is very clearly modelled upon religious experience, and *then* argues that the moral experience we do have is best interpreted as being experience of the moral demand upon us of a really existing God. And Newman fails to see the circularity of his own procedure!

7 The classic introduction to this whole topic is L. A. Selby-Bigge, ed., *British Moralists: Being Selections from Writers Principally of the Eighteenth Century*, 1897, reprinted in the Library of Liberal Arts, New York: Bobbs Merrill, 1964, pp. cii, 423 and 451, all in one volume. See also, more recently, Alasdair MacIntyre, *After Virtue: A Study in Moral Theory*, London: Duckworth, 1981, esp. the opening chapters; and Gertrude Himmelfarb, *The Roads to Modernity: The*

British, French and American Enlightenments, New York: Random House; London: Vintage Books, 2008, with an appreciative introduction by Gordon Brown.

8 *Roads to Modernity.*

9 Revelation 21.22–25.

10 Boulton, *Who On Earth*, p. 176.

11 Robert W. Funk, *Honest to Jesus: Jesus for a New Millennium*, San Francisco: HarperSanFrancisco, Appendix, pp. 326–35.

12 Funk et al., *Gospel of Jesus*, 10.3. From Mark 2.24.

13 Matthew 5.38–42; see Funk et al., *Five Gospels*, p. 143.

14 E.g. the 'prescriptivism' of R. M. Hare, *The Language of Morals*, Oxford: Clarendon Press, 1951.

15 Q/Matthew 7.3; Thomas 26.1–2; Funk et al., *Gospel of Jesus* 13.11–12, p. 63.

16 Luke 18.9–14; Funk et al., *Five Gospels*, p. 369, for commentary.

17 Luke 11.5–8. The commentary on this story in Funk et al., *Five Gospels*, pp. 327f., relates it to the honour/shame culture of the period. I confess that I do read the story in terms of the modern notion of our need to live up to our own ego-ideal, and *not* in terms of the Middle-Eastern ideas about hospitality and shame. My excuse is that the ego-ideal is highly personal, whereas shame is highly public; and the midnight situation is one in which the householder is debating with himself in bed, in the dark.

18 Funk et al., *Gospel of Jesus* 5.1, based on Mark 1.35. But this is clearly only a linking passage devised by the evangelist.

19 Crossan, *Jesus: A Revolutionary Biography*, chs 3, 4.

20 Funk et al., *Gospel of Jesus* 9.3–4; from Q, from Luke 7.33–34. Commentators usually regard Luke as a somewhat better witness to Q than Matthew.

21 Funk et al., *Gospel of Jesus* 2.29–39; most of this passage is from both Q and *Thomas*, and is therefore very well attested.

22 Familiar epigrams in Funk et al., *Gospel of Jesus* 3.15, 16, 17 – all from Q. The most famous parable on this topic is found in *Gospel of Jesus* 4.4–21, with superbly sharp last lines. Then in 4.22f., found in *Thomas* and Mark and Q, and in 4.24–38, from Q, two other good pieces questioning or even ridiculing ordinary ideas of justice. Later, the parable of the two sons, from Luke, is at *Gospel of Jesus* 9.13–31.

Now go through *Gospel of Jesus* with a highlighter, and mark every unit of teaching-tradition that is concerned with questioning the idea of justice. It will become clear that this is the single principal preoccupation of Jesus' moral teaching, which is a big surprise. I take it that he regards our demand for justice as made ugly by the *ressentiment* that so often drives it.

23 Funk et al., *Gospel of Jesus* 7.5, from Q.

24 Funk et al., *Gospel of Jesus* 7.2-4, from Q.

25 Psalm 37.25. The belief in a moral providence that *visibly* works itself out in history has proved remarkably tenacious. It was still defended by Joseph Butler in *The Analogy of Religion* (1736), and even after the Second World War a senior Cambridge historian, Herbert Butterfield, could still see in the fall of the European dictators the working-out of Divine Judgement in history.

26 Funk et al., *Gospel of Jesus* 3.20.

27 John 9.1-3. Compare Luke 13.4, on the fall of the Tower of Siloam. Thus three of the four canonical Gospels report Jesus as acknowledging that the way things go in the world is *not* specially tilted to ensure that the innocent can expect to be protected from undeserved misfortune.

28 Genesis 11.5-9.

29 Funk et al., *Gospel of Jesus* 16.12.

30 Matthew 5.17.

31 For the Lord of the Sabbath saying, see Funk et al., *Gospel of Jesus* 10.34 (from Mark 2.27f.). For Matthew's version of the healing of the paralytic, see Matthew 9.9.

32 Jeremiah 31.33; Ezekiel 36.26.

33 Genesis 2.16-17.

34 Boulton, *Who On Earth*, p. 176.

35 For the Mediterranean world, see Robert J. Miller, *The Births of Jesus and Other Sons of God*, Santa Rosa: Polebridge Press, 2003; and, in India, see also the lives of the Buddha and of Mahavira, the legendary founder of the Jain religion.

36 Funk et al., *Gospel of Jesus*, pp. 11-21.

37 For different reasons both Rudolf Bultmann and a number of Jewish commentators have seen the life of Jesus as having been lived wholly within the history of Judaism.

38 Some early Christian writers saw Jesus as *autobasileia*, 'himself the Kingdom', and it could be that this is the correct interpretation of Jesus' own chosen way of life and his symbolic actions. He *intends* to act out a kingdom which is always coming into being as he goes along, and as others join it and do the sorts of things he does.

39 Albert Schweitzer's 'thoroughgoing eschatology' picture of Jesus scarcely appears at all in Q, in *Thomas*, or in the *Gospel of Jesus*. It seems that all the luridly apocalyptic symbolism came in at the time of the destruction of the Temple in 70 CE, and was used to colour up existing ideas about the Kingdom and about Jesus and his return.

40 There are a few Christian writers who might be thought of as continuing Jesus' satirical style: Erasmus, in *The Praise of Folly*, is

one example. Jonathan Swift, Sydney Smith and Ronald Knox are others worth considering.

41 As in the parable of the Pharisee and the tax-collector, Funk et al., *Gospel of Jesus* 13.5–10.

42 Funk et al., *Gospel of Jesus* 2.36f.; 13.2–4.

43 Funk et al., *Gospel of Jesus* 2.29–35.

44 Funk et al., *Gospel of Jesus* 13.3. It is striking that in a period of extreme reverence for the Holy Name of God (i.e. Yahweh) Jesus endorses the standard view, and never uses the Holy Name himself at all: but then he jumps to the opposite extreme and uses the impossibly cosy expression *Abba*! R. W. Funk, in his note (*The Gospel of Jesus*, 1999 edn, pp. 99f.), finds 'a hint of humour' in this. Compare a well-known passage of St Paul about the divine Spirit testifying with our spirit and leading us to say 'Abba' (Romans 8.15f.). Where the thought of both Jesus and Paul is in its highest flight, God is completely internalized within the human self. He is our own self-consciousness, and could not be more 'intimate'. It is possible, then, that we should regard the term 'Abba' as usable when God has died – that is, fully disappeared into the human heart.

45 See my *The Old Creed and the New*, London: SCM Press, 2006, chapters 15, 16.

46 My ideas in this paragraph, I have to confess, are not wholly original. They arose in my mind when bits of G. E. Lessing became interwoven with some lines from the young Hegel.

47 The chief Old Testament passage about all this is Isaiah 14.12–15, which refers to a widespread ancient myth. Based upon the fading of Venus when the sun rises, the story related how an inferior deity aspired to usurp the throne of the supreme God, and was punished by being expelled from heaven. Venus, the 'daystar', is the only 'star' bright enough to remain visible for a while in daylight. In Greek it is 'phōsphoros', and the title is applied to Christ, not only in Revelation, but also in 2 Peter 1.19.

48 Funk et al., *Gospel of Jesus* 11.1–9, from Mark 3, with relevant parallels in *Thomas* 55, 99 and 101.

49 Funk et al., *Gospel of Jesus* 14.6–10, from Mark 7, with parallels in *Thomas* 14 and Matthew 15.

50 Donne uses the important but scarce word 'eyebeames' in his love poem 'The Extacie'.

51 See the important Q passage (Q/Luke 11.33–36), in Kloppenborg et al., *Q/Thomas Reader*, p. 53, especially for the parallel between the eye and a lamp.

52 1 Samuel 16.7; 2 Corinthians 4.16.

53 See the commentary in Funk et al., *Five Gospels* on Matthew 6.19–20, pp. 150f.

54 On the return of Jesus in our modern post-ecclesiastical Christian culture, see my *The Meaning of the West*, London: SCM Press, 2008.

55 See n. 35, above.

56 Deuteronomy 30.19; Jeremiah 21.8, etc.

57 Luke 22.30, assigned by Kloppenborg to Q – and perhaps ending Q. Funk and the Jesus Seminar were dubious, because this saying and its parallel in Matthew presuppose knowledge of Jesus' coming ordeal. See Funk et al., *The Five Gospels*, p. 389.

58 See Fidel Castro, *El Hombre Nuevo*, the late-1960s book in which the Cuban revolutionary leader described the plan to produce in Cuba a new human being for a new society.

References and Further Reading

T. J. J. Altizer, *The Contemporary Jesus*, Albany, NY: State University of New York Press, 1997.

David Boulton, *Who On Earth Was Jesus? The Modern Quest for the Jesus of History*, Winchester and Washington: O Books, 2008.

Joseph Butler, *The Analogy of Religion, Natural and Revealed, to the Constitution and Course of Nature*, 1736.

Herbert Butterfield, *Christianity and History*, London: Bell, 1949.

John Dominic Crossan, *The Historical Jesus: The Life of a Mediterranean Jewish Peasant*, San Francisco: HarperSanFrancisco, 1991.

— *Jesus: A Revolutionary Biography*, San Francisco: HarperSanFrancisco, 1994.

Don Cupitt, *The Old Creed and the New*, London: SCM Press, 2006.

— *Above Us Only Sky: The Religion of Ordinary Life*, Santa Rosa, CA: Polebridge Press, 2008.

— *The Meaning of the West*, London: SCM Press, 2008.

Emil L. Fackenheim, *The Religious Dimension in Hegel's Thought*, Chicago: University of Chicago Press, 1982.

Robert W. Funk, *Honest to Jesus: Jesus for a New Millennium*, A Polebridge Press Book, San Francisco: HarperSanFrancisco, 1996. See especially the Appendix, pp. 326–35.

R. W. Funk and the Jesus Seminar, *The Gospel of Jesus, according to the Jesus Seminar*, Santa Rosa, CA: Polebridge Press, 1999.

R. W. Funk, Roy W. Hoover and the Jesus Seminar, *The Five Gospels: The Search for the Authentic Words of Jesus*. A Polebridge Press Book, New York: Scribner, 1996.

R. M. Hare, *The Language of Morals*, Oxford: Clarendon Press, 1951.

Gertrude Himmelfarb, *The Roads to Modernity: The British, French and American Enlightenments*, New York: Random House; London: Vintage Books, 2008.

Roy W. Hoover, ed., *Profiles of Jesus*, Santa Rosa, CA: Polebridge Press, 2002.

Geoffrey Keynes, ed., *Blake: Complete Writings*, Oxford: Oxford University Press, 1966.

John S. Kloppenborg, *Q Parallels: Synopsis, Critical Notes and Concordance*, Sonoma, CA: Polebridge Press, 1988.

John S. Kloppenborg and Others, *Q/Thomas Reader: The Sayings Gospel Q and The Gospel of Thomas*, Santa Rosa, CA: Polebridge Press, 1990.

William Langland, *The Book Concerning Piers the Plowman*, tr. Donald and Rachel Attwater, Everyman's Library, 571, London: J. M. Dent, 1957.

Alasdair MacIntyre, *After Virtue: A Study in Moral Theory*, London: Duckworth, 1981.

Robert J. Miller, *The Births of Jesus and Other Sons of God*, Santa Rosa, CA: Polebridge Press, 2003.

— ed., *The Apocalyptic Jesus: A Debate*, Santa Rosa, CA: Polebridge Press, 2001.

— ed., *The Complete Gospels*, paperback edn., San Francisco: HarperSanFrancisco, 1994.

John Henry Newman, *The Grammar of Assent*, 1870.

Reinhold Niebuhr, *An Interpretation of Christian Ethics*, London: SCM Press, 1936.

E. P. Sanders, *The Historical Figure of Jesus*, Harmondsworth: Penguin, 1993.

Albert Schweitzer, *The Quest of the Historical Jesus*, First Complete Edition, ed. John Bowden, London: SCM Press, 2000.

Bernard Brandon Scott, *Reimagine the World: An Introduction to the Parables of Jesus*, Santa Rosa, CA: Polebridge Press, 2001.

L. A. Selby-Bigge, ed., *British Moralists: Being Selections from Writers, Principally of the Eighteenth Century*, 1897, reprinted in the Library of the Liberal Arts, New York: Bobbs-Merrill, 1964.

Geza Vermes, *Jesus the Jew*, London: Collins, 1973, etc.

W. H. Walsh, *Hegelian Ethics*, London and New York: Macmillan, 1969.

Index